# The U.S. Presidency

Look for these and other books in the Lucent Overview series:

# The U.S. Presidency

## by Don Nardo

LUCENT
B·O·O·K·S

GREENWOOD LIBRARY

**Library of Congress Cataloging-in-Publication Data**

Nardo, Don, 1947-
    The U.S. Presidency / by Don Nardo.
        p.   cm. — (Lucent overview series)
    Includes bibliographical references and index.
    Summary: Examines the origins of the U.S. presidency and how
it fits into the American system of government, as well as the many
roles the president plays.
    ISBN 1-56006-157-X (alk. paper)
    1. Presidents—United States—Juvenile literature. [1. Presidents.]
I. Title.   II. Series.
JK517.N37   1995
353.03'13—dc20                                    94-40040
                                                       CIP
                                                        AC

Copyright © 1995 by Lucent Books, Inc.
P.O. Box 289011, San Diego, CA 92198-9011
Printed in the U.S.A.

# Contents

# Introduction

WITH HIS ELECTION in November 1992 and inauguration in January 1993, Bill Clinton of Arkansas became the forty-second president of the United States. The new chief executive brought with him into office his own personal talents, skills, beliefs, and ideals. He also put together a group of advisers, secretaries, and other subordinates, all of whom he felt had their own talents and abilities to contribute to the country. Using these attributes, Clinton hoped to deal effectively with the specific problems and challenges the United States faced in the early 1990s. In a similar manner, each of his predecessors assumed this most powerful political office with his own unique set of attributes. Indeed, the individual personalities, skills, problems, and challenges of the earlier presidents were all very different. So it is not surprising that the quality of their performances as national leaders varied enormously.

## Measuring presidential performance

In fact, while some earned reputations as great presidents, others are remembered by historians, scholars, and political experts as average, fair, or even poor leaders. It is important to note that the yardstick these experts use to measure presidential performance is historical rather than contem-

*(Opposite page) Citizens crowd the U.S. Capitol in 1993 during the inauguration of Bill Clinton, the forty-second president of the United States.*

7

porary. In other words, historical greatness is not the same as public popularity. A president might be extremely popular while in office but later be judged only an average leader because he achieved little of lasting importance. By contrast, a president who is widely opposed and criticized while in office might be seen in the light of history as a great and important leader. Franklin D. Roosevelt, the thirty-second president, is a case in point. Roosevelt served as president during two bleak periods in U.S. history: the Great Depression of the 1930s and World War II. Roosevelt's policies, aimed at lifting the country out of the financial disaster of the depression and at engaging Americans in a war that many wanted to ignore, fostered much criticism. As political scientist James P. Pfiffner explains:

> Franklin Roosevelt is consistently seen as one of the great presidents, primarily because of his moral leadership and vision in leading the country through the traumas of the Great Depression and World War II. When he was in office, however, he was opposed by a significant portion of the political system because his policies were seen as hostile to business interests and as giving too much economic power to the federal government. His conviction that the U.S. had to enter World War II on the side of the Allies encountered serious opposition in the Congress and in isolationist attitudes in the [general] population. Only the Japanese attack on Pearl Harbor galvanized the country for war. . . . Yet, in retrospect, there is a consensus [agreement] across the political spectrum [from liberals to conservatives] that FDR was a great president.

### Ineffective presidents

At the other extreme, the general consensus among experts is that Warren G. Harding, who served from 1921 to 1923, was a highly ineffective president. Both a 1948 *Life* magazine poll of 55 presidential scholars and a 1962 *New York*

*Warren G. Harding has been judged by historians to be the least effective chief executive in U.S. history. Though well-meaning, he lacked leadership skills and good judgment.*

*Times Magazine* poll of 75 scholars rated Harding's performance a "failure." Similarly, two 1982 polls, one by the *Chicago Tribune* of 49 leading scholars, the other a survey of 953 historians by a Pennsylvania State University professor, listed Harding as the worst U.S. president. Harding's poor reputation is easily understandable. He naively appointed social companions, many of whom were inept and untrustworthy, to important cabinet positions and other posts. The government became riddled with corruption and scandal at the highest levels and Harding lacked the skill, decisiveness, and courage to clean his political house. As a result, his administration achieved little and brought shame to the presidency.

Harding was not the only president with a poor reputation. Ulysses S. Grant, who served as presi-

*Richard M. Nixon delivers his farewell speech at the White House shortly before resigning the presidency on August 9, 1974. Nixon was the first president to resign from office.*

dent from 1869 to 1877, also ran an administration wracked by corruption. Not surprisingly, most of the same polls ranked Grant as the second-worst president.

The historical view of presidential performance is not always as clearcut as with Harding and Grant. Historians are sometimes divided on a president's legacy. For example, Richard M. Nixon resigned the presidency in disgrace in 1974 because of his attempt to cover up the 1972 break-in of the Democratic Party's national headquarters in the Watergate complex. The Watergate scandal and Nixon's controversial handling of the Vietnam War probably explain his rating by the 953 historians in the 1982 survey as the third-worst president in U.S. history. And yet, historians also credit Nixon with some major foreign policy achievements including improving diplomatic relations with the communist regimes of the Soviet Union and China.

## Our nation's great presidents

If scandal, corruption, and disgrace made some presidents historically weak and ineffective, what factors made others great? The 1948 and 1962 polls listed Abraham Lincoln, George Washington, Franklin Roosevelt, Woodrow Wilson, and Thomas Jefferson as the five greatest chief executives. Both 1982 polls did the same, with the exception of replacing Wilson with

*Abraham Lincoln discusses the Emancipation Proclamation with his cabinet members. The 1863 document freed the slaves during the Civil War and helped establish Lincoln as one of the nation's most influential and effective chief executives.*

Theodore Roosevelt. One factor all of these leaders shared was that they served with distinction during times of great national crisis or challenge. Scholar Erwin C. Hargrove comments in *The Power of the Modern Presidency:*

> One of the attributes of greatness was an extraordinary talent at leadership in a period of enormous change in American history to which the leader made a creative contribution. Each of the greats was president at a critical time in history and each came through with a lasting solution.

Thus, for successfully steering the nation out of the depths of the depression and through the rigors of a world war, Franklin Roosevelt earned his mark of greatness. Lincoln earned his by coura-

*Crowds cheer Franklin D. Roosevelt at the Democratic National Convention in 1936. Roosevelt's effective leadership during the Great Depression and World War II earned him a lasting reputation as one of the finest presidents.*

*Ronald Reagan was a conservative president who attempted to stimulate economic growth by reducing cumbersome government regulations. He is remembered for his engaging speaking style.*

geously holding the country together during the crisis of the Civil War. And Washington and Jefferson boldly and effectively met the challenge of guiding the country through its formative stages, times of uncertain political experimentation and huge economic and territorial expansion.

It is still too early for the experts to place the performances of the most recent presidents in historical perspective. So, how history will judge Ronald Reagan, George Bush, and Bill Clinton remains to be seen. Reagan, the most conservative president since the 1920s, stimulated economic growth partly by eliminating government regulation of business and industry. Bush enjoyed widespread popularity for leading the United States and its allies to victory over Iraq in the 1991 Persian Gulf War. And Clinton boldly tackled the formidable goals of overhauling the nation's health care and welfare systems. Only time will tell where these or other accomplishments will place these leaders in the rankings of future presidential polls.

# 1

# The Origins of the U.S. Presidency

*(Opposite page) George Washington takes the oath of office in 1789, becoming the first U.S. president. Washington could not have foreseen at the time that the American presidency would eventually become so important in world affairs.*

ON APRIL 30, 1789, George Washington, age fifty-seven, climbed out of a cream-colored coach and strode up the steps of Federal Hall in New York City, the temporary capital of the infant United States. He had become a national hero by leading the rebellious colonial forces in the American Revolutionary War. Now, as massive crowds cheered, he took the oath of office to become the first president of the United States. Afterward, Washington kissed the Bible and, as cannons fired a thirteen-gun salute, he walked to the Senate chamber to deliver his inaugural address.

This marked the beginning of the office of the U.S. presidency. It would, in time, become the best-known and most powerful political office in the world. Each succeeding president would alter and shape the office according to the dictates of his own experiences and personality. So the presidency would grow and evolve over the years, adjusting in new and unique ways to the changing nature and needs of the country and of the world.

Yet the office was decidedly unique even as Washington began his first term. As an institution of national leadership, the fledgling presidency already differed radically from those of other

15

countries, both existing and previous. In large degree, this was because the American founders had created a radically different kind of nation. The government the founders fashioned in the 1780s was the world's first modern democracy. In a world where most peoples still obeyed the whims of absolute monarchs, Americans had instituted an experiment in which the government was an expression of the *people's* desires. This unique system demanded a special kind of leader, one who would wield considerable power but who would still be responsive to the people's needs. In shaping this special kind of leadership office, U.S. founders carefully examined existing and previous kinds of leadership. They accepted those attributes they found admirable, rejected those they thought corrupt or worthless, and then added their own new ideas to the mix.

**The need for a chief executive**

This process of shaping the presidency was just a part of the arduous task of creating a new government for the country. To this end, fifty-five delegates representing the thirteen original states met in Philadelphia in May 1787 in what became known as the Constitutional Convention. Their goal was to reshape and improve the existing national, or federal, government. The system then in place operated under a loose and largely weak set of laws and rules called the Articles of Confederation, which had been established on March 1, 1781. The chief deficiency of the Articles was that they vested all the power in a relatively slow-working national legislature—the Congress. They did not provide for an overall administrator, or chief executive, who could swiftly and decisively carry out the legislature's domestic and foreign policies. As political scholar Neal R. Peirce explains:

The nation's experience under the Articles of Confederation, which provided for no executive department whatever and rested on the principle of equal voting power for all states, large or small, had tended to confirm the delegates' misgivings about leaving all authority in the hands of a legislature. Under the Articles, Congress had shown serious inability to deal with crucial issues like taxation, Western lands, the regulation of commerce, paper money, and Indian affairs. The problem was not only in getting effective legislation passed but in implementing it once it was approved. With no executive to entrust with implementation of laws, the Congress itself had to attempt the job.

Getting dozens of legislators to agree and act together to implement policy proved to be a laborious and sometimes hopeless process. Founder Thomas Jefferson, who would later become the nation's third president, summed up the problem, saying, "Nothing is so embarrassing as the details of execution. The smallest trifle . . . occupies

*The nation's founders meet at the 1787 Constitutional Convention in Philadelphia with the aim of creating an effective working government for the nation. The nature and powers of the chief executive were among their main concerns.*

[Congress] as long as the most important action of legislation. . . . The most important propositions hang over from week to week and month to month, till the occasion have past them and the thing [is] never done."

## The examples of the past

Realizing that the government would remain weak and ineffective without a chief executive, the founders set out to create one. This was no simple process, however. Because the founders had differing opinions about how to structure the nation's highest office, it took them many weeks of intense research, argument, and debate to reach a final agreement. For ideas and inspiration about national leadership, they drew upon a number of sources. The first source was historical example; that is, how various other nations had dealt with the issue of choosing leaders. In plain fact, the vast majority of peoples up to that time had had no choice at all in who led them. Most of the world's rulers had been kings, emperors, and other absolute monarchs whose word was law. The democratic-minded founders rejected this tradition outright.

A few nations had constituted exceptions to the rule of absolute monarchy and the founders deemed these worthy of examination. The first was the ancient Greek city-state of Athens, where democracy was born in the sixth and fifth centuries B.C. Athens had a legislature in the form of an assembly of citizens that debated and voted upon laws. It also had administrators, known as archons, to implement those laws. The problem was that at any one moment the city had several different archons, each entrusted with a different government department. The situation was akin to a modern president's cabinet secretaries— state, treasury, labor, and so on—but without the

president to oversee the various department heads. So the archons often tended to disagree and to overshadow one another, resulting in frequent indecisiveness and inefficiency.

The American founders viewed the leadership setup in ancient Rome more favorably. The Roman Republic, which lasted from 509 to 27 B.C., had two chief administrators called consuls. They carried out the policies of a three-part legislature composed of two assemblies and a senate. But the Republic was not a true democracy because the wealthy senators used their money and influence to control both the assemblies and the consuls. So, the consuls were often mere puppets of the senate, and Rome was actually an oligarchy, a government ruled by an elite group of individuals. The U.S. founders believed that if the Roman consuls had possessed the power to veto, or re-

*The ancient Greek city-state of Athens, depicted here in the second century, created the world's first democracy.*

ject, some of the senate's proposals, the Republic would have been more democratic and might have lasted longer.

The historical example on which the founders concentrated most of their attention was that of the mother country they had recently broken away from—Britain. Since Britain was a monarchy, its supreme leader, at least in theory, was the king, George III. In reality, however, the king was largely subservient to Parliament, the nation's legislature, which over the preceding few centuries had gained political control. Still, the king was the figurehead who represented and spoke for the wealthy and privileged British nobles who controlled Parliament. In a very real sense, then, eighteenth-century Britain was an oligarchy like republican Rome.

*A meeting of the early Roman Senate, whose wealthy, powerful members largely controlled state policy by influencing Rome's two chief executives, the consuls.*

*King George III, who assumed the British throne in 1760 and reigned during the American Revolution in which Britain's American colonies gained their independence.*

Although the Americans had recently fought a bloody war to separate themselves from Britain's monarchy, most founders saw numerous merits in the British system. For instance, they liked the basic idea of Parliament—that is, an elected legislature—and adopted that concept in creating the U.S. Congress. What U.S. leaders did not like was the idea of a privileged monarch who ruled for life, although a tiny minority of the founders still clung to this idea. The aristocratic Alexander Hamilton, for example, advocated an American version of monarchy as the only way to ensure a strong chief executive.

*The British House of Commons as it appeared in 1741. The "Commons," as it is casually referred to in Britain, constitutes one branch of Parliament, the other being the House of Lords. Parliament was the primary model for the U.S. Congress.*

Hamilton's plan, presented in a five-hour speech on June 18, 1787, was the most extreme proposal concerning a strong executive offered at the Constitutional Convention. Hamilton said, "The general power whatever be its form if it preserves itself, must swallow up the state powers, otherwise it will be swallowed up by them." Calling the British system of government "the best in the world," Hamilton doubted "whether any thing short of it would do for America." He also doubted whether a good executive could ever be established "on Republican [completely democratic] principles." A hereditary monarch such as the one in Britain, Hamilton reasoned, possessed great wealth. Therefore, he was above corruption and was "both sufficiently independent and sufficiently controlled [by Parliament or Congress]."

Hamilton did not believe a monarch should be a dictator. But he, like many of his colleagues, did not trust the idea of putting too much power in the hands of the "common people." Most U.S. founders were well-to-do landowners, a kind of American aristocracy, who saw everyday people as lacking the education and breeding to make important political decisions. According to this view, the people should have the right to voice their likes, dislikes, and needs through voting. But weighty matters of state should rest in the hands of a chosen few. Hamilton believed that a kind of controlled monarchy, in which these few would balance the power of a benevolent ruler, was best for the nation.

But Hamilton found himself at odds with most of his colleagues. George Washington summed up the general view in a letter to fellow founder John Jay of New York, declaring:

*Alexander Hamilton, who argued at the Constitutional Convention for creating an American monarch whose powers would be balanced and contained by the legislature. The majority of Hamilton's colleagues rejected this idea.*

What astounding changes a few years are capable of producing. . . . Even respectable characters speak of a monarchical form of government without horror. From thinking proceeds speaking; thence to acting is often but a single step. But how irrevocable [unchangeable] and tremendous! What a triumph for the advocates of despotism [dictatorship] to find that . . . systems founded on the basis of equal liberty are merely ideal and fallacious [false]! Would to God that wise measures be taken in time to avert the [surely dire] consequences.

Washington was no doubt relieved when, repelled by the idea of an American king, the delegates rejected and did not even vote upon Hamilton's proposal.

### Theory and practical application

The founders drew upon more than historical examples in their creation of a national chief executive. They were also strongly influenced by the writings of well-known political thinkers of the preceding two centuries. Seventeenth-century English philosopher John Locke's *Two Treatises on Government*, for example, seemed particularly relevant to the situation the founders faced. Locke argued strongly for separation of governmental powers—that is, dividing authority between the legislature and a chief executive so that the two powers balanced each other. That way neither could hoard too much power and become dictatorial. It might be "too great a temptation," said Locke, "to human frailty [weakness] apt to grasp at power, for the same persons who have the power of making laws, to have also in their hands the power to execute them."

Another reason a powerful executive was needed, said Locke, was because legislatures tended to work too slowly, a fact the weak performance of the Articles of Confederation had already made clear to the founders. According to

*English philosopher John Locke. His writings, which advocated separating government branches such as the legislature and chief executive, strongly influenced the U.S. founders.*

Locke, the executive should have "the power to act according to discretion [personal judgment], for the public good, without the prescription of the law, and sometimes even against it." In other words, the executive should be able to act quickly and decisively in an emergency. The legislature, Locke stated, is "too slow" and cannot foresee and provide for "all accidents and necessities that may concern the public." Locke's arguments confirmed the founders' belief that they needed an administrator separate from Congress who could swiftly execute the laws created by that body.

The founders realized that while such political theory was valuable, observing a practical application of these ideas would be even more valuable. Seeing an example of an executive in action would show how such a leader used, and perhaps abused, various specific powers. But in a world

*The nation's founders debated the merits of balancing the powers of the chief executive and the legislative body. This balance was intended to prevent the president or Congress from gaining too much power.*

dominated by monarchs, where could they find a working example of the kind of democratically elected chief executive they envisioned? Luckily, the precedent they sought existed in the person of George Clinton, the first governor of New York State. Clinton was a talented and courageous leader and New York's brand-new constitution gave him many of the powers the founders were considering for the national chief executive. Scholar Louis Koenig explains that Clinton's

> powers all foreshadowed the [U.S.] presidency. The governor was commander-in-chief and "admiral of the navy," he could convene the legislature on extraordinary occasions, and he could grant reprieves and pardons. His duty was to inform the legislature of the condition of the state, recommend matters for their consideration, and take care that the laws were faithfully executed. . . . The

governor shared . . . veto power with a Council of Revision [consisting of himself and the state supreme court judges]. They, or any three of them, always including the governor, could veto legislative measures inconsistent with the spirit of the constitution or the public good.

## How much power?

The founders had considered historical examples of rulers, the writings of political theorists, and the working model of New York's governor. Next, they began to debate what specific powers to give the country's chief executive. (They had decided that this chief executive would bear the title of president.) Several delegates agreed that the president should have many of the same powers possessed by New York's George Clinton. He should, for instance, have whatever authority was needed to enforce the nation's laws. And he should be commander in chief of the military so that he could quickly quell domestic disturbances or defend the country against foreign aggression. All of the delegates agreed with Locke's principle of separation of powers and therefore that the president's authority should be carefully balanced with that of the legislature. As New York's distinguished statesman Gouverneur Morris put it, "Make him too weak: the legislature will usurp [seize] his power. Make him too strong: he will usurp the legislature."

In general, the delegates split into two camps. The first, which included Hamilton and Morris, advocated a strong, authoritative president. They felt that the president, like the New York governor, should have the power to veto all laws passed by the legislature. This, according to Morris, would cast the president in the role of protector of the common people against the potential tyranny of the legislators. Morris stated:

*U.S. founder George Clinton served with distinction as governor of New York, an office to which he was reelected six times.*

One great object of the executive is to control the legislature. The legislature will continually seek to aggrandize [empower] and perpetuate themselves; and will seize those critical moments produced by invasion or convulsion [domestic disaster] for that purpose. It is necessary then that the [president] should be the guardian of the people, even of the lower classes, against legislative tyranny, against the great and the wealthy who in the course of things will necessarily corrupt the legislative body. Wealth tends to corrupt the mind and nourish its love of power, and to stimulate it to oppression. . . . The executive therefore ought to be constituted as to be the great protector of the people.

In contrast, some delegates feared that giving the president too much power would only lead to an executive, rather than a legislative, form of tyranny. Among the members of this more cautious group were Connecticut's Roger Sherman and New Jersey's William Paterson. Some of their

*Founders Roger Sherman of Connecticut (left) and William Paterson of New Jersey argued for a presidency with limited powers in order to avoid the chance of executive tyranny.*

proposals advocated having the president's powers checked by an advisory council or even suggested having multiple presidents in the manner of the Roman consuls. Paterson's plan called for the president's selection by Congress, which could remove him at will. The chief executive would have no veto or war-making powers, thereby ensuring that he could never abuse his power and influence.

## The Constitution's safeguards

Eventually, the founders settled on a plan that fell midway between the two extremes. The president they provided for in the Constitution was a single executive chosen by election rather than by Congress. He had a significant set of powers, including those of commander in chief and the legislative veto. He also had the important power to appoint Supreme Court judges, diplomats, and other important public figures.

But the founders carefully built into the Constitution a number of safeguards to check their executive's powers. Following the ideas of Locke and other writers, they created a system in which governmental power was balanced among the president, Congress, and Supreme Court. As founder James Madison of Virginia put it, "The great security against a gradual concentration of the several powers in the same department consists in giving to those who administer each department the necessary constitutional means and personal motives to resist . . . the others. Ambition must be made to counteract ambition." Thus, the Constitution provided that while the president could check congressional power through the veto, Congress could check executive power by having sole authority to make laws and to assign how the nation's money would be used. And although the president had authority to appoint Supreme Court judges, Supreme Court judges could in turn check the president's power by declaring his actions unconstitutional and therefore illegal.

The founders also provided in the Constitution for the president's term of service. This had been the subject of much argument and debate during the Convention. At one extreme, Hamilton and Morris had advocated allowing the executive to serve for life, providing he was fair and effective. Other, more cautious, delegates—among them Thomas Jefferson—had suggested a single presidential term of a few years with no chance of re-election. Eventually, the founders settled on a four-year term with unlimited chances of re-election. The degree to which many founders worried about potential executive tyranny is seen by Jefferson's immediate misgivings about this final compromise. In November 1787 he wrote to fellow founder John Adams that a president with unlimited terms is, in effect,

> an officer for life. . . . Once in office, and possessing the military force of the union . . . he could not easily be dethroned, even if the people could be induced to withdraw their votes from him. I wish that at the end of 4 years they had made him forever ineligible [for] a second time [in office],

As it turned out, Jefferson benefitted from the unlimited re-election policy outlined in the Constitution. Two decades later, when he himself was president, he was glad to have the opportunity to run for a second term. (In the late 1940s, after Franklin Roosevelt's four terms in office, Congress adopted a two-term limit on the presidency.)

### A man of shrewdness and integrity

The constitutional provisions for the presidency constituted a well-constructed blueprint for the nation's highest office. But the office was as yet untested. The first elected president had yet to

*During his service as president from 1789 to 1797, George Washington did much to shape the new office, including creating the first presidential cabinet.*

prove that the founders' careful plans were workable. More importantly, the first chief executive would have the chance to grow in the office, to test the limits of his constitutional powers, and perhaps to set policy in areas the Constitution did not address. Upon his election, George Washington fully realized that his every action would set a precedent that would affect his successors. "I walk on untrodden ground," he said. "There is scarcely any part of my conduct that may not hereafter be drawn into precedent."

Indeed, Washington's presidential actions and precedents did nearly as much to define the office for future generations as did the framework in the Constitution. One of his most significant achievements was the creation of a cabinet composed of the heads of the government's most important departments. The Constitution had not mentioned the concept of an executive cabinet. Washington

*Members of Washington's cabinet, including Thomas Jefferson and Alexander Hamilton, attend one of the regular cabinet meetings called by the first president. This practice became a tradition followed by all later presidents.*

wisely delegated many important tasks to his cabinet members, all extremely capable individuals such as Secretary of State Thomas Jefferson, Secretary of the Treasury Alexander Hamilton, and Attorney General Edmund Randolph. Toward the end of his first term, the new president began to call the cabinet members together in regular meetings, a practice his successors would follow.

Washington also created lasting presidential policy in his dealings with Congress. Many expected him to become directly involved in legislative debates and bickering. But he shrewdly remained aloof from the Congress, giving his office a certain level of dignity and prestige, and delegated battles with legislators to Hamilton and other subordinates. Equally important, by his example Washington showed that the president could and should show restraint in using his considerable powers and influence. Washington used his veto power only twice. And he retired to private life after his second term, though his popularity would have easily assured him a third if he had chosen to run again.

In addition, Washington tried to set an example of presidential honesty, a precedent he earnestly hoped later chief executives would follow. "His integrity was most pure," Jefferson observed, "his justice the most inflexible I have ever known. . . . He was indeed, in every sense of the words, a wise, a good and a great man." Unfortunately, only some of Washington's successors managed to live up to the ideal of goodness he set. Yet, through both theory and practice, the first president and his fellow founders left behind a strong, effective, and highly flexible national executive office, one that would stand the test of time. The U.S. presidency has already endured for over two centuries, a period in which more than forty men have sworn the same oath that Washington did on April 30, 1789:

> I do solemnly swear that I will faithfully execute the office of the President of the United States, and will to the best of my Ability, preserve, protect and defend the Constitution of the United States.

# 2

# Selecting the President

THE AMERICAN FOUNDERS envisioned the selection of the president as a fairly simple process and created a specific procedure for that purpose. Over time, however, the trials and errors of practical experience revealed flaws in the system, problems they had to correct by changing the Constitution. The original selection process also had an important philosophical flaw. Instead of allowing the general citizenry to select the president directly, through the ballot box, the founders designated a chosen few to pick the country's highest leader. Therefore, the process was largely undemocratic. The Congress eventually corrected this flaw, although some questions still remain about the fairness of the solution.

Over the course of time, the presidential selection process changed in other ways that the founders did not foresee. It became increasingly longer and more complex and today consists of a host of customs, traditions, and public events spanning more than a year prior to the actual voting. These include political parties, national nominating conventions, extensive and costly campaigns, debates, and heavy media coverage. Though these elements have come to be seen as natural parts of

*(Opposite page) George Bush delivers his acceptance speech at the 1988 Republican National Convention, at which he received the nomination to run for president. Such nominating conventions are an important part of the long, complex presidential selection process.*

35

the political landscape, it should be noted that none of them existed in the nation's early years. Thus, presidential selection, like the office itself, is an evolving process that has changed and will likely continue to change over time.

## The electoral college

The starting point of that evolution was at the 1787 Constitutional Convention, in which the delegates argued, debated, and eventually agreed upon how the office of president would work. They suggested a number of ways that the chief executive might be selected. Two proposals, one giving the choice to Congress and the other allowing the people to choose directly in a national election, inspired much debate. The delegates decided against the first idea because it gave the Congress too much power over the president and therefore undermined the principle of separation of powers.

The delegates rejected the concept of direct election because they did not trust the general populace with such an important decision. Some of the aristocratic founders referred to the public as a "great beast." They feared that a democracy that gave the public too much direct power would be weak, chaotic, and eventually would fail. As Alexander Hamilton put it, "When the deliberative [decision-making] or judicial powers are vested wholly or partly in the collective body of the people, you must expect error, confusion and instability." This was why the founders made only one of the two legislative wings, the House of Representatives, open to direct popular election. Members of the other wing, the Senate, were originally chosen by the state legislatures. Since these bodies were largely composed of educated, well-to-do, upper-class individuals, they could be counted on to select senators from their own

ranks, men who would work to contain the excesses of the popularly elected House members.

Eventually, a special committee of the Constitutional Convention's delegates worked out an alternative presidential selection plan agreeable to nearly everyone. The plan introduced the electoral college. This was not a school of higher learning but instead a special group of presidential electors, a few located in each state, whose task was to vote on and select the president. The founders wanted the electors who would vote for president to be educated men of good character and breeding like themselves. To ensure this, they rejected the idea of having the electors chosen in a popular election. Instead, as in the case of senators, the state legislatures would choose the electors. According to James Pfiffner:

> The number of electors from each state would be
> equal to the combined number of representatives

*The U.S. House of Representatives, depicted in session in 1868. At first, this was the only legislative body with members chosen by popular election. By contrast, the founders provided for senators to be chosen by the state legislatures in order to counter possible "excesses" by the house.*

*A special congressional session is convened to count the electoral vote in a nineteenth-century U.S. election. The electors themselves met and voted in their respective states.*

and senators of each state. In order to preclude cabals [secret deals] and conspiracies, the electors would not meet together but separately in their states. After voting, the results would be forwarded to the Congress for counting. In order to prevent undue influence of the incumbent [sitting] government, no member of the national government could be an elector. To be declared the winner, a candidate would have to receive a majority of the votes. Lacking a majority, selection of the president would be made by the House of Representatives voting by state [each state having one vote].

The plan also provided that the candidate who came in second would automatically be declared vice president.

Under this original electoral system, the link between the president and the general citizenry was indirect and minimal at best. Only a minority of adult white males, mainly those who owned property, could vote. They elected the state legislators, who in turn chose the electors, who in turn chose the president. Because only a select few of the citizenry had a say in picking the nation's leader, the system was not very democratic. But the founders sincerely, if naively, believed that the wisdom and goodwill of that select few would ensure a fair and efficient selection process.

## A constitutional crisis

However, the leaders of the infant United States soon found that their electoral system did not work quite as well as they had hoped. The first problem arose because of the unexpected emergence of political parties in the early 1790s during Washington's first term as president. The country's leaders polarized into two parties—the Republican (which later evolved into today's Democratic Party) and the Federalist. The Republicans, led by Madison and Jefferson, advocated that the government should respond strongly to the people's needs and desires. The Federalists, led by Hamilton and Adams, argued for a more detached government that largely decided what was good for the people. The two groups organized because each feared where the policies of the other might lead the country.

The founders had failed to foresee how this development might affect the electoral process. In the election of 1796, John Adams, a Federalist, won the electoral vote and became the nation's second president. Thomas Jefferson came in second, making him vice president. But Jefferson was also a Republican, which meant that the two chief executives, who were supposed to work closely with each other, belonged to opposing parties. Not only was this an embarrassing situation, it was also politically divisive. Jefferson, who increasingly believed the Federalists might erode the freedoms guaranteed in the Constitution, openly worked to undermine some of Adams's policies.

An even worse flaw in the electoral system revealed itself in the 1800 election. The Republicans had chosen Aaron Burr of New York to run as their vice presidential candidate with Jefferson. But the electoral college cast a tie vote—seventy-three ballots each—for Jefferson and Burr. This created the nation's first constitutional crisis. As the election passed into the House of Representatives, where legislators are free to choose any candidate they want, the disturbing possibility arose that a vice presidential candidate might defeat his own presidential running mate. Even worse, the opposition candidate, John Adams, who had not received a majority in the original

*Due to flaws in the electoral system, John Adams found himself serving with a vice president who belonged to the opposing political party.*

voting, might be chosen. After thirty-six suspenseful ballots, the House finally chose Jefferson as president and Burr as vice president, as the Republicans had intended in the first place. But the need for an amendment revising the constitutional electoral process was now clear to all. Congress passed this rules change in 1804. In his book *American Presidents and the Presidency*, historian Marcus Cunliffe states:

> The Twelfth Amendment—specifying that the electors were to cast two distinct ballots, one for president and one for vice president—was fashioned in Congress, passed onto the states and duly ratified, in time to ensure that Thomas Jefferson was reelected to the presidency in 1804, and that his vice president was of the same political persuasion. On this occasion the oft-renewed precedent was set: the vice president . . . while a man of reasonable standing, was selected not because he was considered of presidential timbre [quality] but because he could lend geographical or other support to the ticket.

### An illusion of the popular will

Despite the Twelfth Amendment, potential problems with the electoral system remained. Although the general population took part in presidential elections, the results were essentially meaningless, as it was the electoral voting that actually chose the country's leader. Few people complained as long as the winner of the popular vote was the same person chosen by the electors and as long as the system gave the illusion of reflecting the popular will. The election of 1824 abruptly shattered this illusion. Tennessee's Andrew Jackson received ninety-one electoral votes, along with a plurality, or higher total than anyone else, in the popular vote. But Jackson's electoral total was not a majority and the Constitution stipulated that a candidate had to receive a majority

*New York's Aaron Burr received the same number of electoral votes as Thomas Jefferson in the election of 1800. The House of Representatives finally broke the tie, declaring Jefferson president and Burr vice president.*

*Though he had received more electoral and popular votes than his opponents, Andrew Jackson lost the 1824 election when the House chose John Quincy Adams over him.*

of electoral votes to win. This once more threw the election into the House. There, the political forces of the second- and fourth-place finishers in the electoral voting—John Quincy Adams and Henry Clay—combined to oppose Jackson. The House ended up choosing Adams, who had received only 30 percent of the popular vote, as compared to Jackson's 43 percent.

## Electoral reform

Because of this extremely unpopular decision, Americans at all levels of society began demanding electoral reform. Thanks to the influence of Jackson and other strong political leaders, by 1832 all states had eliminated the selection of electors by the state legislatures. Instead, the electors were now chosen by direct popular election. Having the everyday voters choose the electors, who would in turn choose the president, gave the people a more direct say in presidential selection and was therefore more democratic. The states also adopted the "unit rule." This provided that any candidate receiving a plurality of a state's popular vote would automatically receive all of that state's electoral votes.

With only a few minor revisions, the 1830s' version of the electoral system has survived to the present. Many Americans today labor under the mistaken impression that they choose the president and vice president directly in the general election. In reality, the electors still do the crucial voting. The two major parties, the Democrats and Republicans, each choose a list of potential electors in each state for the upcoming election. If a state is entitled to ten electoral votes, for instance, ten Democratic electors and ten Republican electors are nominated and put on the ballot. By casting a ballot for the Democratic candidate, the voter is actually choosing the ten Democratic electors and, in a sense, instructing them under the unit rule to cast their votes for the Democratic candidate.

Some political writers and leaders believe that the electoral system of choosing the president is still imperfect. This is because the possibility remains that a candidate might receive the most popular votes and still lose the election. First, he or she might not receive a majority of electoral votes. In that case, the election will go into the House, which could conceivably pick someone who garnered only a minority of popular votes.

The other way this unwanted scenario could happen is through the random occurrence of voting within the states. This could happen in an election in which the Democratic and Republican candidates are running neck and neck, each having the same number of popular and electoral votes. States A and B, which have fifteen and twenty electoral votes, respectively, are the last to vote. The Democrat receives 500,000 popular votes in state A to the Republican's 400,000 and gets the state's fifteen electoral votes. The Republican receives 520,000 votes in state B to the Democrat's 500,000 votes, giving the Republican state B's twenty electoral votes. The Democrat receives a total of 1 million popular votes for the two states and the Republican 920,000. So in the direct popular vote, the Democrat wins the national election by a margin of 80,000 votes. But because state B has 5 more electoral votes than state A, the Republican wins the electoral vote and with it the presidency.

Although this has not actually happened, it has come very close to reality on several occasions: in 1948, in the race between Harry S Truman and Thomas Dewey; in 1960, in the race between John F. Kennedy and Richard M. Nixon; and in 1976, in the election between Gerald Ford and Jimmy Carter. Such close calls, James Pfiffner

*A political ticket advertising the candidates and electors for the Whig Party in Ohio in the 1836 election. Harrison lost to Democrat Martin Van Buren.*

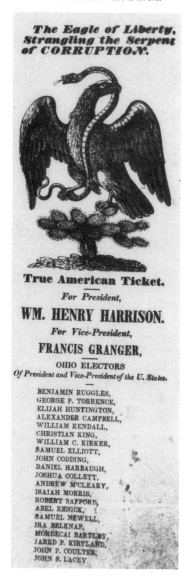

**The Eagle of Liberty, Strangling the Serpent of CORRUPTION.**

**True American Ticket.**

*For President,*

**WM. HENRY HARRISON.**

*For Vice-President,*

**FRANCIS GRANGER,**

OHIO ELECTORS
*Of President and Vice-President of the U. States.*

BENJAMIN RUGGLES,
GEORGE P. TORRENCE,
ELIJAH HUNTINGTON,
ALEXANDER CAMPBELL,
WILLIAM KENDALL,
CHRISTIAN KING,
WILLIAM C. KIRKER,
SAMUEL ELLIOTT,
JOHN CODDING,
DANIEL HARBAUGH,
JOSHUA COLLETT,
ANDREW M'CLEARY,
ISAIAH MORRIS,
ROBERT SAFFORD,
ABEL RENICK,
SAMUEL NEWELL,
IRA BELKNAP,
MORDECAI BARTLEY,
JARED P. KIRTLAND,
JOHN P. COULTER,
JOHN S. LACEY.

writes, have led some critics to argue that the "Electoral College system is an accident waiting to happen."

## A reluctance to tamper with the system

Opponents of the electoral system have periodically tried to institute a constitutional amendment that either drastically revises or totally eliminates the electoral college. In the course of the nation's history, over five hundred such proposals have been introduced in Congress. The debate surrounding such a proposal in 1956 was particularly spirited. At a Senate hearing on the matter, Senator John Pastore of Rhode Island, who wanted to toss out the electoral system, explained his position this way:

> I want to do away with the Electoral College. I want to elect my president on election day. I say that when the people go to the polls the man who receives the greatest number of votes should be elected president of the people.

Senator John F. Kennedy of Massachusetts spoke in support of the electoral college, which Congress retained by a large margin. In explaining his position, Kennedy offered the same reasons all supporters of the electoral system cite. First, direct election might undermine the two-party system by encouraging numerous small parties to run and thus spreading the vote thinly among many candidates. In theory, the winner might receive as little as 10 percent of the votes and not really represent the will of a significant proportion of the people. Also, say supporters of the electoral system, direct election might allow the states with the largest populations to decide the election outcome. This would give these states too much power over the others. The 1956 proposal, said Kennedy, "while purporting to be democratic, would increase the power of and en-

*As a U.S. senator in the 1950s, John F. Kennedy strongly supported the existing electoral system. He believed that direct election of the president would encourage the formation of a confusing, divisive array of small political parties.*

courage splinter parties and I believe it would break down the federal system under which most states entered the Union, which provides a system of checks and balances to ensure that no area or group shall obtain too much power."

To date, all other similar proposals have failed to gain the political support necessary to initiate the constitutional amendment process. Thus, even after two centuries, most American lawmakers remain reluctant to tamper too much with the imperfect but practical and workable system the founders created.

While the voting aspect of the presidential selection process changed only slightly over the years, other aspects of the process underwent

*Delegates attend the Democratic National Convention on July 4, 1868, in New York City. The appearance and growth of such conventions mirrored the increasing participation of the masses in the political process.*

enormous change. The presidential nomination process, for example, originally occurred completely behind closed doors. A small group of congressional leaders held a caucus, or private meeting, in which they chose the nominees for president and vice president.

Over time, as increasing numbers of Americans gained the right to vote and became involved in the political process, nominating the president became a public show. In the 1830s, the first national party conventions were held. These huge meetings, in which thousands of people heard speeches by and demonstrated their support for the candidates, quickly became a cherished American tradition. Every four years, each major party held a convention to pick its candidates. However, the actual selection of the nominees remained largely an undemocratic process as the congressional caucus gave way to the "smoke-filled room" of the party caucus. Often, powerful political bosses made secret promises and deals in order to line up votes for their favorite candidates.

Eventually, demands for reform of this unfair system became widespread. Responding to the cries of "No more boss rule!" and "Down with King Caucus!" in 1903 Wisconsin became the first state to pass a "primary law." Within ten years, all other states had switched to the primary election system. In a primary election, held many months before the main election, the voters either choose the nominees by direct ballot or choose delegates who, in turn, choose the candidates at the national conventions.

### Presidential campaigning

Another fundamental change in the process of selecting the president was the growth of the presidential campaign. At first, when nominating and voting for the chief executive was the province of a chosen few in Congress and the electoral college, no one saw any need for campaigning. But with the growth of political parties and popular participation in politics, this changed rapidly. Candidates began to travel from city to city, making speeches to crowds of prospective voters. Rival candidates or their supporters attacked each other verbally, in newspaper interviews, and in leaflets and posters. They also occasionally debated each other, as Abraham Lincoln and Stephen Douglas did in their famous 1858 encounters, each of which had an audience of several thousand people. Still, without the mass media of radio and television, the average candidate could personally reach only a small fraction of the voters. Before the twentieth century, most

*Gerald Ford campaigns in the 1976 election. In modern presidential campaigns, the mass media give the voters a close, penetrating view of the candidates.*

Americans never had the opportunity to see or hear the candidates and had to rely on what they read or heard about them.

## Swaying the voters through the media

The advent of mass media for the first time gave the voters a real feeling for the candidates' personalities and these innovations became integral parts of presidential campaigns. In the 1930s, Franklin D. Roosevelt effectively exploited radio by giving regular "fireside chats," in which he talked directly and frankly to the American people. The caring, fatherly image he gained was a contributing factor in his unprecedented string of four presidential victories (1932, 1936, 1940, and 1944). Since that time, all candidates and sitting presidents have used the medium of radio.

*Abraham Lincoln (at podium) and Stephen Douglas (standing directly behind Lincoln) debate in one of their legendary 1858 encounters. Though dramatic and important, at the time only a few thousand voters could witness such events.*

In the 1950s, television added a new dimension to the presidential selection process. Millions of voters could simultaneously see the candidates, live and up close, a situation in which the slightest hint of weakness or insincerity could seriously hurt a candidate's image. The power of the new medium was demonstrated in the first-ever televised presidential debates in 1960. The participants were the Democratic candidate, John F. Kennedy, and his Republican opponent, Richard M. Nixon, the sitting U.S. vice president. According to presidential historian Forrest McDonald:

*Beginning in 1960, presidential debates were televised, reaching tens of millions of viewers. Here, Democratic candidate John F. Kennedy (far left at podium) and Republican candidate Richard M. Nixon (seated at far right) engage in one of their four televised encounters.*

> That vice president Nixon consented to take part in the debates showed that he did not yet understand the impact of television. He could easily have begged off, saying that the dignity of his office precluded his taking part in meaningless exercises, but he had prided himself on his talents as a

*Republican president George Bush (left), Democratic candidate Bill Clinton (right), and independent candidate H. Ross Perot debate in 1992. In such encounters, the camera captures and magnifies the candidates' slightest mistakes or moments of indecision.*

debater since high school, and he accepted Kennedy's challenge. . . . Although opinions differed as to who won, Kennedy came across as having far the more attractive personality, and television is a personality medium. Thus Nixon dissipated [lost] in one hour the advantage he had had as the experienced statesman running against the inexperienced youth.

Television remains an essential and powerful ingredient of the presidential campaign process, one that can sway the feelings of millions of voters in a few seconds. In a 1992 televised presidential debate, for instance, sitting president George Bush, the Republican candidate, confronted Democrat Bill Clinton and independent

H. Ross Perot. While an opponent was speaking, Bush casually looked at his watch. Many viewers interpreted this as a sign of Bush's disinterest or nervousness and the media generally gave Clinton the victory in the debate.

The American founders did not foresee the advent of television and other mass media and how these inventions would affect the process of picking the national leader. Similarly, they did not anticipate party conventions, popular primaries, and national campaigns. Given the conditions that existed in their day, they did their best to create a selection process that worked. Despite far-reaching changes in the world, the country, and American politics, as well as modifications in the basic system, that system is still in place and still works. And that testifies to the greatness of the founders' achievement.

# 3

# The President as Legislative Leader

THE AMERICAN FOUNDERS established the doctrine of separation of powers with the idea that the Congress and the president would share power and have clearly defined roles. According to the Constitution, Congress's job is to make the laws and the president's is to make sure they are carried out. The Constitution is silent, however, on which governmental branch should suggest or draft prospective legislation. Thus, while the president has no power to pass a law, he is perfectly free to suggest one and ask that the legislators pass it. But most early presidents were not very active in the legislative process. During the nation's first century, the Congress drafted, as well as passed, nearly all legislation. As a result, in the nineteenth century, Congress largely dominated the government and overshadowed the president, particularly in the area of domestic affairs.

This situation changed dramatically in the twentieth century. Major participation in the legislative process became one of the hallmarks, along with vigorous leadership in foreign affairs and as commander in chief, of a strengthened

*(Opposite page) President Bill Clinton addresses a joint session of Congress. Over the course of the nation's history, the chief executive's role has become increasingly important in the creation of legislation.*

53

presidency. The transformation from relatively weak chief executives to increasingly stronger ones began with Theodore Roosevelt, who first took office in 1901. Roosevelt's famous remark, "Oh, if I could be president and Congress too for just ten minutes," summed up his belief that the slow-working legislature often impeded the president from getting things done. If a president wants certain laws passed, he advocated, he should take the legislative initiative. "A good executive under the present conditions of American political life," he remarked, "must take a very active interest in getting the right kind of legislation." Roosevelt took just such an active interest in suggesting legislation. And later presidents, especially Woodrow Wilson and Franklin D. Roosevelt, became highly involved in the lawmaking process. In fact, they and their successors assumed such an active role in legislative leadership that historians often refer to the twentieth century as the era of the "legislative presidency." In this

*Theodore Roosevelt set the tone for the "legislative presidency" that came to dominate the Congress in the twentieth century.*

era, with few exceptions, the president's power and prestige have largely overshadowed those of the Congress.

## The trial-and-error method

The founders did not foresee the exact nature of this power struggle between Congress and the president. But they clearly anticipated that one branch might try to dominate the other. That is precisely why they carefully defined and separated the various governmental powers in the Constitution: to keep one branch from gaining too much power. In the realm of lawmaking, explains James Pfiffner, the founders

> gave the legislative power to the Congress. Article I, Section 1, provides that: "All legislative powers herein granted shall be vested in a Congress of the United States. . . ." Section 8 of Article I enumerates [lists] the . . . powers of Congress and gives Congress the power "To make all Laws which shall be necessary and proper. . . ." The president's legislative powers are minimal. Article II provides for the President to inform Congress on the state of the union, to recommend "necessary and expedient" measures to Congress, to convene both Houses on extraordinary occasions, and to adjourn them in cases of disagreement between them. The Constitution also gives the president the power to veto legislation, the most important formal power of the president in the legislative process.

Thus, outside of the veto power, the founders did not expect the president to become very involved in lawmaking procedures. At first, their expectation was fulfilled, even regarding the veto. George Washington vetoed only two bills in his eight years as president, and John Adams and Thomas Jefferson refrained from using the veto at all in their total of twelve years in office. The same can be said for efforts by the early presidents to draft legislation. Washington suggested only three specific laws to the legislature and did

*Thomas Jefferson tried to influence Congress by gaining the backing of key congressional leaders but did not formulate legislation himself.*

not submit complete, detailed, and legally worded drafts of these bills.

Jefferson took a more active legislative role than either Washington or Adams, but still did so only indirectly. Using his considerable personal persuasive powers, Jefferson got the backing of many congressional leaders, who then developed legislation he favored. And some of his cabinet secretaries actually helped these lawmakers formulate legislation. But the president himself refrained from direct attempts to dominate Congress by originating the bulk of legislation. No doubt he and his predecessors were reluctant to do so partly because they were still unsure of the best way to balance their powers with those of Congress. The country's first decades, says presidential historian Wilfred E. Binkley, "may be looked upon as a period of . . . trial-and-error . . . [in] the relationship between the executive and the legislature."

## Opening the door to the legislative presidency

For the most part, the nineteenth-century presidents who followed this formative period continued to be inactive in the legislative process. Some, particularly those who served in the 1840s, did so because they held the philosophical view that Congress should be supreme. Others simply lacked the strong leadership qualities needed to challenge and dominate Congress. The major exception was Abraham Lincoln. He aggressively initiated numerous important laws and, reacting to the extreme crisis of the Civil War, employed a set of controversial "emergency powers" that allowed him to dominate Congress and the government. But Lincoln's assassination in the beginning of his second term suddenly halted the shift toward presidential dominance that he had begun. Between his death and Theodore Roosevelt's election, a string of weak chief executives occupied the White House, and Congress largely dominated national politics.

Roosevelt opened the door to what would eventually become the legislative presidency by challenging and setting an agenda for Congress. As Forrest McDonald puts it:

> Roosevelt, in his State of the Union messages, directed attentions to the new conditions [the country faced] and called for an active federal response. He insisted that there must be "progressive regulation" of "our gigantic industrial development," and toward that end proposed . . . tougher antitrust laws, banking and currency reform, immigration restriction, conservation of natural resources . . . and similar measures.

Using both facts and figures and his tough, forceful personality, Roosevelt persuaded many congressional leaders that his legislative ideas were

*Abraham Lincoln visits the Union camp at Antietam, Maryland, during the Civil War. To deal with the war, Lincoln assumed a number of emergency powers that allowed him to overshadow Congress.*

essential and thereby got many of them passed. However, he was careful not to upset the established order in Congress for fear of alienating the legislators he had won over. As a result, he was somewhat reluctant to become involved in the actual drafting of every bill, commenting on one occasion, "Are you aware of the extreme unwisdom of my irritating Congress by fixing the details of a bill, concerning which they are very sensitive?"

## Setting a strong example

The man who entered the White House in 1913 was not so concerned with congressional sensitivities. He was Woodrow Wilson, who, in walking through the door Roosevelt had opened, boldly challenged Congress's legislative dominance. An astute student of history, Wilson had observed the weakness of the presidency in the nineteenth century. He believed that many of the ineffective presidents failed to set a strong example and thereby win the people's trust. If a president "rightly interprets the national thought and boldly insists upon it, he is irresistible," he wrote in 1908. "And the country never feels the zest of action so much as when its president is of such insight and caliber. . . . A president whom [the nation] trusts cannot only lead it, but form it to his own views."

In Wilson's mind, the only effective way to shape the country to his views was through vigorous legislative leadership. According to Louis Koenig:

> Far more than most presidents, Woodrow Wilson was deeply involved personally in the legislative struggle. As a political scientist and an admirer of British public affairs, he had long been convinced that the president must be a kind of "prime minister, as much concerned with the guidance of legislation as with the just and orderly execution of law." Wilson oversaw the development of a body

*Woodrow Wilson was the first chief executive to submit detailed drafts of legislative bills to Congress.*

of legislation promoting economic and social justice, the "New Freedom." He believed that only the president could ensure an integrated legislative program. Wilson, therefore, regularly planned it, shared in the toil and sweat of drafting bills, and oversaw their progress through Congress.

Thus, one way that Wilson made sure the kind of legislation he favored became law was by providing detailed drafts of bills and working directly with his supporters in Congress until the bills passed.

## Congress's feet put to the fire

When Congress resisted him, Wilson used another method, one Theodore Roosevelt had used on occasion. Wilson, more often and more forcefully than Roosevelt, took his case directly to the people. He called together journalists from major newspapers and magazines and explained in detail why a particular bill he advocated was important.

*Lyndon B. Johnson signs the Civil Rights Housing Act on April 11, 1968. Johnson was an expert at gaining public support for his policies.*

An unusually earnest individual who believed in the moral superiority of his own views, Wilson was often able to win the support of a public already eager for economic and social reform.

Thereafter, many other presidents used this tactic. One of the most effective was Lyndon Johnson, who served from 1963 to 1969. After leaving the presidency, Johnson wrote:

> When traditional methods fail, a president must be willing to bypass the Congress and take the issue to the people. By instinct and experience, I preferred to work from within, knowing that good legislation is the product not of public rhetoric but of private negotiations and compromise. But sometimes a president has to put Congress's feet to the fire.

Johnson went to the people several times in order to get important civil rights legislation passed. Conservative southern legislators, reluctant to allow blacks equal rights with whites, resisted him on the Civil Rights Act of 1964, the Voting Rights Act of 1965, and the Housing Act of 1968. In televised speeches to the American people, Johnson characterized such resistance as old-fashioned, unfair, and un-American. Newspaper and television polls showed that a majority of voters had been moved by the president's pleas and the bills passed.

Some later presidents have taken their legislative agendas to the people on a more regular basis. In this regard, Bill Clinton has done so more than most. When Congress is seriously considering the merits of an important bill he has submitted, Clinton, along with many of his cabinet secretaries and other close supporters, goes "on the road" to drum up public support. His favorite media arena is the "town meeting." Clinton stands

*President Bill Clinton answers questions in one of his regular town meetings. Taking the chief executive's views directly to the people has become a popular tool of the modern legislative presidency.*

before a small audience of townspeople, answers their questions, and tells why the pending bill is so vital. Immediate and numerous replays of his remarks usually follow on the news shows and C-SPAN, ensuring that a majority of Americans hears his message. In this way, Clinton has tried to follow the lead of strong legislative presidents before him.

### An avalanche of legislation

But while Roosevelt and Wilson pioneered the legislative presidency, it was Franklin D. Roosevelt, Theodore's cousin, who perfected it and firmly established the modern presidency's dominance over Congress. Like Lincoln, Roosevelt was elected at a time of supreme national crisis. When Roosevelt took the oath of office on March 4, 1933, the nation was severely crippled by the enormous economic depression that had begun with the great stock market crash of 1929. Hundreds of U.S. banks had failed, causing large numbers of Americans to lose their life savings. Millions of people were out of work and destitute, and the farming industry, basis of the country's vital food production system, was on the verge of collapse. Roosevelt believed that the only way to save the nation was through massive emergency legislation. And the only way to get a great deal done quickly was for him to take complete charge—to formulate the legislation, draft it, coordinate it, and push it through Congress using any means necessary. He stated his intentions clearly in his inaugural address, saying:

> It is to be hoped that the normal balance of executive and legislative authority may be wholly adequate to meet the unprecedented task before us. But it may be that an unprecedented demand and need for undelayed action may call for temporary departure from the normal balance of public procedure. . . . In the event that Congress shall fail

*Franklin D. Roosevelt reacted to the crisis of the Great Depression by developing a massive volume of emergency legislation and forcefully influencing and manipulating Congress to pass it.*

*Citizens line up to receive a one-cent meal during the Great Depression of the 1930s. Franklin Roosevelt's legislative measures helped to bring the nation out of the crisis.*

to take [the necessary] courses and . . . the national emergency is still critical I shall not evade the clear course of duty that will then confront me.

With breathtaking swiftness, the new president backed up his words with action. In the first one hundred days of his term, which proved to be the single most productive lawmaking period in U.S. history, Roosevelt forced an avalanche of legislation through Congress. For a time, that body became almost literally the president's rubber stamp. As James Pfiffner tells it:

Immediately after he was sworn into office . . . Roosevelt declared a bank holiday and, on March 9, called the Seventy-third Congress into special session to pass the Emergency Banking Act. Over the next 100 days, Congress passed a flurry of laws meant to deal with the economic crisis. All of the bills save one were drafted in the White House, with occasional participation by members of Congress, and while some amendments were considered, none of the proposals emanating from the White House was fundamentally changed. The president, for the first time, was acting as a prime minister in controlling the legislative agenda and directing the legislative process.

In the remainder of his first term, Roosevelt continued to dominate Congress. He used a variety of tools to achieve success: the appointment of talented, energetic assistants to help him formulate and draft legislation; the force of his authoritarian yet congenial personality to bend legislators to his will; the continual use of his veto power to frustrate opponents (he vetoed 635 bills, a large number even for a president who served four terms); the frequent and skillful use of public press conferences to get his messages out; and the artful exploitation of radio to build a relationship of trust between himself and the American peo-

*Franklin Roosevelt delivers a radio fireside chat in which he outlines his opinions and solutions to the problem of economic inflation.*

ple. In a sense, Roosevelt almost single-handedly created the modern presidency. "He brought to the presidency a phenomenal combination of understanding, temperament and ability," says scholar David Mervin, "that enabled him to build on the groundwork provided by Theodore Roosevelt and Woodrow Wilson in consolidating and massively expanding the president's legislative role." After Roosevelt, initiating legislation and guiding it through Congress became the expected and routine way for presidents to create and maintain their domestic policies.

### Roosevelt's shadow

While modern presidents still largely overshadow Congress, none of Franklin Roosevelt's successors have managed to match the sheer size and scope of his legislative legacy. This is perhaps partly because none of the more recent presidents has had to react to a crisis as overwhelming as the Great Depression. Nevertheless, some modern presidents have been much more effective legislative leaders than others. This has been due to a number of factors, among them the fact that each executive has faced a different set of problems. Also, some presidents have lacked the skills needed to be strong legislative leaders. Others—Richard Nixon and George Bush, for instance—emphasized foreign over domestic policy, and so were not as successful in creating a wide range of legislation. According to Forrest McDonald, "Nixon was not especially interested in legislation or in the legislative process. He talked about domestic policy from time to time . . . but he appeared to Congress to lose interest quickly." Whatever the reasons, both Nixon and Bush failed to take full advantage of the power of the legislative presidency and as a result did not build strong and durable domestic policies.

By contrast, a few modern presidents have demonstrated considerable success in manipulating Congress and the legislative process. Invariably, these were the leaders whose domestic policies had far-reaching and long-lasting effects. For example, in shaping the historic civil rights laws of the 1960s, Lyndon Johnson forced the nation to overhaul its outdated social and legal systems, which discriminated against African Americans. This legislation profoundly affected and continues to affect people on all social levels. In the early 1980s, Ronald Reagan used his formidable communication skills to win the trust of a majority of Americans. "In his expert hands," remarks David Mervin, "television and radio [became] invaluable weapons essential to his success in gathering support for his policies." With this strong public support, Reagan managed to push a large and unusually conservative agenda through Congress. Under his leadership, the legislature passed the largest tax cut in history, as well as the biggest increases in peacetime defense spending.

That the legislative presidency is still a powerful feature of the modern U.S. government is well illustrated by Bill Clinton's vigorous legislative initiatives in his first two years in office. Up against equally vigorous opposition in Congress, in 1993 he won important legislation designed to lower the national deficit over a period of many years. He also oversaw passage of the North American Free Trade Agreement, or NAFTA, which will help shape the country's international business dealings for decades to come. In addition, Clinton has committed his administration to the monstrous task of overhauling the nation's cumbersome and costly health care system. If he is successful, the achievement may be comparable to some of Roosevelt's and Johnson's great triumphs of social legislation.

*Lyndon Johnson's social policies, especially the civil rights legislation he initiated beginning in 1964, had long-lasting effects on American life.*

*Ronald Reagan addresses the United Nations General Assembly. The legislation he initiated, including a huge increase in defense spending, helped to bolster the economic boom of the 1980s.*

Whatever the outcome of his legislative efforts, Clinton and those who follow him will always have to face the fact of living and working in Roosevelt's shadow. In the area of legislative leadership, Mervin points out, "Roosevelt has been the standard against which his successors have inevitably been measured."

# 4

# The President as Commander in Chief

A PRESIDENT'S POWER as commander in chief, or highest ranking official, of the U.S. military makes him the most formidable military opponent in the world. The president and his secretary of defense, both civilians, are followed in the chain of command by the joint chiefs, or heads of the various service branches. These include the army, navy, air force, and marines. In times of war or military emergency the president discusses strategy with the defense secretary and joint chiefs. But, as commander in chief, the president has the final word on the deployment and use of all troops, equipment, and weapons, including the country's huge nuclear arsenal. Presidents have used this vast military authority not only to defend the country, but also to enforce various kinds of national or international policy.

Yet the president does not possess constitutional power to commit the nation to war. Only Congress has the authority to actually declare war. Over the course of U.S. history, however, most presidents did not hesitate to use the military in undeclared conflicts, both small and large. In

*(Opposite page) In the role of commander in chief, President Nixon visits American troops in Vietnam in 1969. The U.S. presidency commands a vast array of troops and weapons, making it the most powerful military office in the world.*

nearly all of these incidents, a significant proportion of legislators maintained that the president had overstepped his constitutional authority. On more than one occasion, Congress attempted by various means to block the president's military policies or to force him to consult the legislature before making important military decisions. These moves were largely unsuccessful. The debate over which government branch should have a larger share of war powers is certain to continue into the next century.

**The concept of civilian supremacy**

The controversy over the constitutional powers of the country's commander in chief began in the 1787 Constitutional Convention. The first issue the founders discussed in this regard was whether to give the office of president command of the nation's military forces. More to the point, should they entrust such command to a serving military leader or to a civilian? Looking at historical examples, the founders saw that supreme military commanders in other lands were nearly always either kings, generals, or admirals. And this, the founders perceived, was what made these lands dictatorial and undemocratic—that both monarchy and military held all the power—and with it overshadowed and controlled the people. American leaders wanted to create a government in which power rested in the people's hands. They wanted to ensure that ambitious generals could not, as they had so often in other lands, abuse their power by taking over the government. The best way to do this, the founders concluded, was to take the unprecedented course of vesting supreme military authority in a civilian. And as chief administrator entrusted with enforcing the country's laws, the president was the most logical choice for the role of commander in chief.

But as logical and commendable as this plan seemed at the time, it was not yet proven by actual experience. Would military leaders actually follow a civilian's orders? No one expected this to be an issue in the nation's first few years. There was little doubt in anyone's mind at the time that George Washington, the immensely popular and respected head of the former revolutionary forces, would become the first president. Military men would surely follow his orders happily and to the letter. But what about later, when a person who was not popular or who had never served in the military became commander in chief? Only when such a leader had a major confrontation with one of his generals and prevailed would the founders' plan ultimately prove sound and practical.

*George Washington takes command of the rebel army during the American Revolution. Later, as civilian commander in chief, Washington easily maintained the respect and loyalty of the troops.*

Eventually, such confrontations between presidents and their subordinates did occur and showed the founders' plan to be both wise and workable. According to Article II, Section 3 of the Constitution, the president "shall commission [appoint] all the officers of the United States." Unstated but understood in this phrase was the idea that the president could fire as well as hire these officers. Removing a general who commanded enough men and resources to march on Washington, D.C., and take over the government constituted a true test of a civilian commander in chief's authority. One of the most dramatic of such incidents occurred on November 5, 1862, when Abraham Lincoln relieved General George B. McClellan of his command. The president felt that McClellan had not exploited his battlefield opportunities and advantages vigorously enough. A tense moment followed, in which some of McClellan's

*Abraham Lincoln meets with General George B. McClellan at Antietam. Later, after the president relieved him of his command, McClellan briefly considered marching his army against the federal government.*

*President Harry Truman (right) meets with General Douglas MacArthur before the confrontations that led Truman to fire the famous military hero.*

officers urged him to disobey Lincoln. The general actually considered marching his 120,000 troops on the capital. But the moment passed. In an elaborate and solemn ceremony, McClellan surrendered his command to General Ambrose E. Burnside.

Perhaps the most famous case of the civilian president exerting authority over his military subordinates was Harry S Truman's removal of General Douglas MacArthur on April 11, 1951. As commander of the U.S. and UN forces in the Korean War, MacArthur, a headstrong and self-righteous individual, repeatedly and publicly questioned Truman's war policies. Truman finally took decisive action in order to preserve presidential authority and civilian supremacy. He wrote to a friend:

> I reached a decision yesterday morning after much consideration and consultation on the Commanding General in the Pacific [MacArthur]. It will undoubtedly create a great furor [public uproar] but under the circumstances I could do nothing else and still be president of the United States.

Truman's action did create an uproar in which many people, both in and out of government, supported MacArthur. But top military officials stood firmly behind the president, who, like Lincoln, had demonstrated the ultimate authority of the civilian commander in chief. "In both episodes," comments Louis Koenig, "civil[ian] supremacy had been maintained over the professional military, a cardinal [important] arrangement of the democratic state."

### Broadly interpreting the Constitution

Another controversial aspect of the commander in chief's constitutional military powers is that he shares them with Congress. The doctrine of separation of powers was foremost in the founders' minds in 1787, and they made certain to apply this doctrine to all areas of government, including the military. Fearing the advent of dictatorship if the president held too much power, they vested sole power to declare war in the Congress. They also gave Congress the power to organize, regulate, and financially support the nations' armies and navies. The founders stated the president's military authority in a single constitutional phrase in Article II, Section 2: "The President shall be commander in chief of the Army and Navy of the United States, and of the militia of the several states when called into the actual service of the United States." To the founders, the meaning of this arrangement was clear. Congress's job was to provide for and maintain the military and decide when to go to war. The president's job was to lead the troops, that is, to carry out a war once it was declared. Under this formula, Congress has declared war and the president carried it out five times in the nation's history. These conflicts included the War of 1812, the Mexican-American War, the Spanish-American War, World War I, and World War II.

However, in practice, most presidents have interpreted the seemingly straightforward wording of Article II, Section 2 very broadly. According to this broad interpretation, as commander in chief the president has two important tasks. The first is to respond quickly to a potential military threat or other disaster when the legislature cannot act or is too slow to act. The second task is to use the military to protect American lives and property. To support this claim, almost all presidents since Lincoln have also cited Article II, Section 3 of the Constitution, which states that the president "shall take care that the laws be faithfully executed." According to Lincoln, the country's laws guaranteed the people's freedom, safety, and property rights. So by protecting these rights, the president was fulfilling his duty to faithfully execute these laws. Using this and equally broad interpretations of various other constitutional passages, Lincoln justified the emergency actions he took to preserve the Union during the Civil War, which was an undeclared conflict. These legally questionable moves included declaring martial law in some areas, ordering people arrested without warrants, and closing post offices for conveying "treasonable" correspondence. According to Forrest McDonald, Lincoln told Congress such actions were necessary

*President Lincoln interpreted certain passages of the Constitution very broadly in order to justify some of the extreme emergency measures he ordered during the Civil War.*

> because he was bound by the Constitution to take care that the laws be faithfully executed, and in the insurrection [Civil War] the "whole of the laws which were required to be faithfully executed were

being resisted and failing of execution in nearly one-third of the states." He justified his action on the ground that he had taken the constitutionally mandated oath to "preserve, protect and defend the Constitution of the United States." The first purpose for which the Constitution was established, according to its preamble, was "to form a more perfect union," and if the president was to preserve and defend the Constitution he must necessarily preserve and defend the Union.

## Presidents as policemen

Since Lincoln's time, presidents have continued to use these same broad interpretations of the Constitution to justify using the military in undeclared conflicts or one-time military expeditions. In all, U.S. presidents before and after Lincoln have ordered the country's forces into harm's way or actual combat in such incidents over 160 times. Two of these undeclared conflicts—in Korea (1950–1953) and in Vietnam (1964–1975)—were full-fledged wars that produced thousands of American casualties. However, the majority of the undeclared incidents were small so-called police actions, which occurred frequently enough for the United States to earn the reputation of appointing itself the "world's policeman." Historian Richard M. Pious explains:

The armed services are used for "police actions" that protect Americans against pirates and bandits, drug traffickers, smugglers, and guerrillas and terrorists. Forces may be ordered to cross borders and make limited incursions into other nations. . . . The president may send the military into other nations to put down mobs threatening American lives and property, or to participate in missions to rescue nationals of various nations. The armed forces may remain for a period of time to police a town or region, or participate in a military occupation according to terms negotiated with the foreign government.

One typical and well-known example of such a police action occurred in 1916. A Mexican bandit named Pancho Villa, who led a small army that opposed the Mexican government, crossed the U.S. border and raided a New Mexico town. President Woodrow Wilson ordered U.S. expeditionary forces under General John J. Pershing to pursue Villa into Mexico, a move the Mexican people and their government deeply resented. Another famous presidential police action took place in April 1980. President Jimmy Carter authorized a secret armed rescue mission to free a group of Americans held hostage in the Middle Eastern country of Iran. The mission ended in failure after three of the eight helicopters involved were lost in a desert sandstorm. And in June 1993, President Bill Clinton ordered a missile attack on a military headquarters in Iraq, also in the Middle East. The assault, Clinton announced, was intended to punish members of the Iraqi military who had conspired to assassinate former president George Bush during a visit to the Middle East a few months before.

*Mexican bandit Pancho Villa (above), whose raid on an American town prompted President Wilson to order a military response by General John J. Pershing (below center).*

*The wreckage of a failed American mission to rescue hostages in Iran is a reminder of secret presidential police action taken in 1980 by Jimmy Carter.*

In these and other police actions, the principal aim of the presidents who ordered them was to protect American lives and property or to punish those who threatened them. But presidents have consistently used their powers as commander in chief, in both declared and undeclared wars, to pursue numerous other goals and policies. For instance, in 1801 Thomas Jefferson sent the U.S. warship *Enterprise* to rid the western Mediterranean Sea of pirates who posed a hindrance to free trade in the area. Under the pretense of protecting American ships, Jefferson later sent a larger naval force. U.S. warships waged an aggressive campaign that almost literally eliminated pirates from the Mediterranean and thereby expanded U.S. economic opportunities in the region.

In 1846, the presidential goal was to expand U.S. territory rather than trade opportunities. The president, James K. Polk, wanted to provoke Mexico into a fight so that he could seize California and other valuable Mexican lands. He not only successfully provoked the confrontation, but also managed to get Congress to legitimize his action by formally declaring war. At the time, says Richard Pious:

> Texas had just joined the Union, Mexico [claiming Texas was still Mexican territory] was threatening war, and Polk placed three thousand troops on alert near the disputed border. Polk reinforced naval units in the Pacific, to be in a position to take the Mexican province of Upper California with its excellent harbor at San Francisco. . . . The president

*James K. Polk succeeded in persuading Congress to declare war on Mexico in 1846. His goal was to expand U.S. territory.*

then ordered General Zachary Taylor into the [disputed] territory. . . . Mexico then declared "defensive war," and some American troops were killed in an engagement. . . . News of the incident enabled Polk to claim that Mexico had invaded Texas.

The result was that Polk got his war and the United States won California and other southwestern lands. But Polk's opponents in Congress, angry over being manipulated into declaring war, forced him in the peace treaty to settle for less territory than he wanted. The House also passed a resolution that condemned Polk for a war "unnecessarily and unconstitutionally begun by the President of the United States."

### Manipulating Congress

The events surrounding the beginning of the Vietnam War in many ways parallel those of the Mexican War, although, in the case of Vietnam, President Lyndon Johnson's basic policy goal was entirely different than Polk's. Rather than seeking new territory, Johnson, serving during the height of the anticommunist "cold war," wanted to prevent the spread of communism in Asia. His goal was to help the non-Communist land of South Vietnam defeat and absorb communist North Vietnam. Johnson, like Polk, used his power as commander in chief to provoke a confrontation and then get congressional support allowing him to escalate hostilities in the area. Johnson claimed that two U.S. ships patrolling in international waters in the Gulf of Tonkin near North Vietnam in August 1964 had been attacked without reason or warning by North Vietnamese forces. In retaliation, the president had ordered an assault on North Vietnamese ships and naval facilities. Believing this version of the events, Congress quickly passed the Tonkin Gulf Resolution.

Though not an actual war declaration, the resolution approved Johnson's use of force, and he then used the document to justify increasing U.S. involvement in the Vietnamese conflict.

Four years later, however, a congressional committee investigated the Tonkin Gulf incident and found that Johnson had presented Congress a slanted version of the events. The committee discovered that the U.S. ships had not been in international waters but rather, in North Vietnamese waters. Furthermore, the ships had entered the area knowing full well that they might be attacked. Therefore, the committee concluded, the president had purposely provoked the incident and misled Congress. Like many other presidents, then, Johnson used his position as commander in chief to pursue national policy and at the same time usurped and manipulated Congress's constitutional powers.

*President Johnson greets U.S. troops in Vietnam in the late 1960s. Johnson used the Tonkin Gulf Resolution to justify escalating U.S. military involvement in southeast Asia.*

Congress eventually fought back in an attempt to reclaim its authority to commit the nation to war. In November 1973, the legislature passed the War Powers Act (or Resolution). It did so partly in response to Johnson's earlier tactics and also to President Nixon's 1970 secret bombing of Vietnam's neighbor, Cambodia, as part of the Vietnam War effort. "In every possible instance," the new resolution stated, the president must "consult with Congress" before committing U.S. troops to combat or situations in which combat is clearly imminent. If the president does commit troops without a formal war declaration, the resolution stated, he must withdraw those troops within sixty days if Congress does not approve the action.

### A blank check to wage war

To the disappointment of many legislators, the War Powers Act has been largely unsuccessful in forcing the president to share his war powers with Congress. First, presidents have managed to sidestep the provision demanding that they consult Congress beforehand by broadly interpreting the term "consult." Most of the time, they merely "inform" Congress a few hours or days before committing troops. For example, in 1975, President Gerald Ford informed congressional leaders that he was sending troops to rescue the U.S. merchant ship *Mayaguez*, which had been captured by a group of Cambodian communists. Since the decision to fight had already been made, Congress found itself in the same role it had played before passing the War Powers Act—that of mere spectator.

Some critics of the War Powers Act have gone so far as to claim that the law actually strengthens the president's military hand. They say it provides him with a blank check to wage war for sixty days without any regard for Congress. As proof,

*U.S. Marines raise the American flag on the merchant ship* Mayaguez *in 1975 after retaking the vessel from the Cambodian communists who had captured it.*

they cite President Reagan's invasion of the Caribbean island of Grenada in 1983 in order to thwart local communist rule. Reagan did not inform Congress before committing troops, so Congress started the sixty-day clock per the provision in the law. However, Reagan knew from the outset that the operation would be a short one. He withdrew the troops in plenty of time to comply with the law and emerged with his mission and overall goal completed, while Congress once more helplessly sat by and watched.

In 1974, scholar Erwin C. Hargrove correctly predicted another potential weakness of the War Powers Act that did not show itself until much later. The law, wrote Hargrove, "fails to recognize

*President Reagan congratulates U.S. Marines who took part in the 1983 invasion of Grenada, a small island in the southern Caribbean.*

*President Bush visits the U.S. Army base in Saudi Arabia in 1990. The base served as the military operations center during the Persian Gulf War against Iraq's dictator, Saddam Hussein.*

that the congressional response to presidential action . . . will depend upon politics, not legality. The rally round the flag factor will predominate. Both Congress and public are likely to stand behind a president [when his cause is popular]." Hargrove's prediction came true in January 1991 when Congress authorized President Bush to use U.S. forces to liberate the tiny nation of Kuwait, which Iraq had overrun in August 1990. Bush had been planning a large-scale invasion of Iraq for months without congressional approval. Many in Congress did not want to give Bush a blank check that might lead to another Vietnam-like conflict. But American and worldwide public sentiments strongly supported Bush's tough military stance. Not wanting to appear as though they were undermining the president, U.S. legislators approved the impending invasion. Once more, the president's ability to overshadow Congress's war powers prevailed.

Regarding war powers, presidents are likely to maintain their edge over Congress, at least for the foreseeable future. The U.S. president now holds a set of military weapons and powers that the founders could never have anticipated. The question is not whether presidents will continue to exploit these resources. They most certainly will. The important question is: Will Congress attempt to modify the War Powers Act and challenge the president for a bigger share of military authority? The only likely way that will happen is if a future president commits what Congress and the people see as a serious misuse of his authority as commander in chief. And such an event is impossible to predict. Until such a time, the president will likely remain, in a very real sense, the most powerful individual on earth.

# 5

# The President and American Foreign Policy

THE PERSON WHO holds the office of president of the United States possesses the most influential voice in world affairs today. This is partly because the United States is the recognized global military superpower and the president, as commander in chief, has immediate control of the U.S. military. The president's international influence also derives from the status of the United States as the world's richest and most industrialized nation. Trade with and/or financial aid from the United States can mean the difference between prosperity and economic hard times for many nations. Thus, how the president conducts foreign affairs directly affects people not only in the United States, but around the world as well.

This has not always been the case. In the first few decades of its existence, the United States was a relatively small economic and military power in comparison to European powers such as Britain, France, and Spain. Had it not been for the great barrier of the Atlantic Ocean and the difficulties of waging war across it, the American colonies might never have succeeded in their war

*(Opposite page) President Reagan meets with Soviet leader Mikhail Gorbachev in 1987. As leader of the richest, strongest nation on earth, the U.S. president exerts profound influence on the fortunes and affairs of foreign nations.*

87

of independence from Britain. Later, that same barrier, along with the Pacific Ocean in the west, contributed to U.S. isolationist attitudes. As late as 1940, most Americans felt separate and distant from the problems and turmoils of foreign countries and desired to stay that way. But the threats to world peace and freedom that sparked World War II inevitably drew the United States into the international fray. In 1945, the country emerged from war as the world's strongest and most economically developed nation, and ever since that time the U.S. president has held the unofficial position of leader of the free world.

Presidents have not held this crucial position entirely alone, however. As in the areas of legislation and war powers, the history of U.S. foreign policy has demonstrated a constant interaction between the president and Congress. Though the president's voice in foreign affairs is clearly the dominant one, Congress regularly succeeds in making its own voice heard. While the president negotiates foreign treaties, for instance, such agreements remain invalid without congressional approval. Sometimes the two branches cooperate on foreign policy matters. But more often they disagree. Thus, in attempting to set the nation's foreign policy goals, presidents regularly find themselves the targets of congressional criticism and opposition.

## Presidents and precedents

Though the Constitution divides foreign policy powers between president and Congress, presidents early began carving out their dominant niche in this area. The first few presidents clearly recognized the importance to the nation of well-negotiated treaties. Such agreements could end wars, form alliances of mutual protection, and decide territorial disputes. The president's treaty-making powers were based on Article II, Section 2 of the Constitution, which gave him the authority "by and with the advice and consent of the Senate, to make treaties, provided two-thirds of the Senators present concur." Thomas Jefferson summed up the opinion of the early presidents that "making" a treaty was a far more important role than "approving" it. Said Jefferson:

> He [the president] being the only channel of communication between the country and foreign nations, it is from him alone that foreign nations or their agents are to learn what is or has been the will of the nation; and whatever he communicates as such, they have the right, and are bound to consider, as the expression of the nation.

Jefferson was so confident of his foreign policy authority that he did not even bother to consult with Congress before or while negotiating treaties. At the time, a number of legislators held that such consultation was called for in the constitutional phrase "with the advice and consent of the Senate." But on this point Jefferson followed George Washington's precedent. According to Richard Pious, at first Washington tried to consult with the Senate:

> He informed the chamber that he wished their advice on a proposed Indian treaty, and then appeared in the Senate. . . . A motion to postpone debate was carried, which infuriated Washington, since he assumed that the senators did not wish to discuss the treaty in his presence. He stormed out of the chamber vowing that he would never return. Several days later, in a tense atmosphere, Washington came back and the Senate offered some advice, but never again did he repeat the procedure.

Thereafter, Washington interpreted the phrase "advice and consent" merely as part of the Senate's approval process. He submitted already negotiated and completed treaties to that body, the practice presidents have followed ever since.

*Thomas Jefferson, like his predecessor George Washington, negotiated treaties without the participation of Congress.*

Since the days of Washington and Jefferson, presidents have continued to assume the dominant role in foreign affairs. This does not mean that Congress's role is unimportant or that the legislature lacks authority to counteract the president. The power to reject a treaty can assert congressional authority and have far-reaching consequences. The most famous case occurred in 1920 when the Senate rejected the Treaty of Versailles, which officially ended World War I. President Wilson had negotiated U.S. participation in the League of Nations, a forerunner of the United Nations, into the treaty's terms. But the Senate was hostile to the idea of the League and refused to approve the treaty. This hurt Wilson's international prestige. Also, lacking U.S. participation, the League was weak and proved unable to solve

*Congress listens to President Wilson as he reads the armistice terms ending World War I. Members of Congress, citing their opposition to a clause providing for the formation of the League of Nations, rejected the treaty that officially ended the war.*

the political and military crises that ultimately led to World War II.

In addition to being able to defeat a treaty by a two-thirds margin, the Senate can force a president to make important changes in a treaty. When Jimmy Carter negotiated a treaty with Panama over the Panama Canal in 1978, for example, he had to make certain changes desired by Congress in order to win its approval. Congress can also launch an investigation of a particular presidential policy or proposal. As part of such an investigation, public hearings can affect public opinion, which can, in turn, sway a president's policy. Also, Congress holds the power of the purse. So by refusing to appropriate money, it can affect a foreign policy program initiated by the president.

However, these congressional advantages are clearly outweighed by those of the president. First, presidents are usually able to gather a great

*President Jimmy Carter (seated, far left) signs the Panama Canal Treaty in 1978.*

deal of public support for their proposed treaties. As political scientist Albert B. Saye explains, "As head of the United States government, [the president's] public statements always command attention, both at home and abroad. Thus he is in a much better position than Congress to exploit the press, radio, and television to mobilize public opinion in support of his positions." As a result, the Senate invariably ends up rejecting very few treaties. Of the more than 1,480 treaties submitted since 1789, only 11 have been rejected. And only about 15 percent have been significantly altered by Congress before ratification. According to Saye, the president maintains other advantages over Congress in foreign affairs:

> He is always on hand, while Congress is frequently not in session. The unity of his office permits him to act swiftly and—if necessary—secretly, something that Congress, composed of several hundred individuals, cannot do. He has superior sources of information on current international developments, and a permanent staff of experts to analyze this information for him. If he desires, he may keep this information secret, or he may release it as he thinks advisable in support of his policies. . . . Because he can act swiftly and secretly, the president can often confront Congress and the nation with a *fait accompli* [a done deal] before there is an opportunity for public discussion.

### The National Security Council

The permanent advisory staff the president maintains is known as the National Security Council, created in 1947. The statutory, or permanent, members of the council are the president, vice president, secretary of state, and secretary of defense. In addition to these vital personnel, the chairman of the military joint chiefs and other officials sometimes attend council meetings. One of the group's functions is to help the president formulate foreign policies.

Another advantage the president enjoys in foreign affairs is unlimited use of executive agreements. These are agreements the president negotiates on his own without any congressional participation. Not mentioned in the Constitution, they constitute an authority that presidents have assumed on their own and legitimized through constant use. In theory, a treaty is a weighty, long-lasting agreement between two or more nations, while an executive agreement is a more informal, temporary agreement. However, in practice, the two have proven to be the same. Presidents sometimes shrewdly use executive agreements in place of treaties. For example, in 1845 the Senate refused to ratify a treaty between the United States and the Republic of Texas which provided for U.S. annexation of Texas. So President John Tyler issued an executive agreement that accomplished this goal. And in 1905, when the Senate did not

*A session of President Johnson's National Security Council in the 1960s. The council is the chief executive's most important single source of advice in the area of foreign affairs.*

*John Tyler, the tenth American president, issued an executive agreement in 1845 providing for the annexation of the Republic of Texas by the United States.*

ratify a treaty with Santo Domingo in the Caribbean, Theodore Roosevelt negotiated an executive agreement that included the same provisions as the treaty. In all, U.S. presidents have issued nearly thirteen thousand executive agreements, the majority of these after 1940.

**Transforming statement into policy**

Other advantages the president maintains in foreign affairs derive from the unique and privileged nature of the presidential office. For instance, because the president holds so much military power and political influence, his public statements carry a great deal of weight and are taken seriously both domestically and abroad. Therefore, sometimes presidents purposely make important policy statements in their speeches. These policies, though in theory not legally binding, can then commit the nation just as firmly as any treaty.

One of the most famous examples of a president setting major foreign policy through a mere public statement was the Monroe Doctrine. In the early 1820s, the United States feared that Spain, Portugal, and other European powers would attempt to interfere with the many Latin American nations (in the Caribbean and Central and South America) that had recently declared their independence. President James Monroe and other U.S. leaders believed that the United States should protect the rights of its weaker neighbors. They also wanted to keep the Europeans from establishing powerful footholds in the Western Hemisphere. So in his annual message to Congress on December 2, 1823, Monroe announced to the world:

*James Monroe initiated the Monroe Doctrine, a policy that warned European and other foreign nations to keep out of North and South American affairs.*

The American continents, by the free and independent conditions which they have assumed and maintain, are henceforth not to be considered as subjects for future colonization by any European powers. . . . We . . . declare that we should consider any attempt on their part to extend their system to any portion of this hemisphere as dangerous to our peace and safety.

Though no documents of any kind had been signed, the meaning was clear: U.S. influence in the Western Hemisphere was supreme. Succeeding presidents staunchly upheld the Monroe Doctrine. By backing it up with the threat of military force, they transformed a statement into a widely respected international policy.

### Power through personal diplomacy

The unique authority the president possesses also allows him to use personal diplomacy, much of it secret, to convince foreign heads of state to act in a certain manner. "For the president," remarks Louis Koenig, "power in foreign affairs lies in the ability to persuade foreign leaders, whether friend or foe or neutral, to back his policies." The importance of such diplomacy was aptly illustrated during the Cuban missile crisis in 1962. When the United States learned that the Soviets had installed nuclear missiles in Cuba near the U.S. mainland, a tense confrontation followed, in which President John F. Kennedy publicly demanded that the Soviets remove the missiles and the Soviets refused. Kennedy finally resorted to secret personal exchanges with Soviet leader Nikita Khrushchev. According to Koenig:

The Kennedy-Khrushchev exchanges opened up an understanding that averted general war. An essential feature of the arrangement was the secrecy. . . . Personal communication permitted greater privacy and was less susceptible to leaks than regular channels, and, unlike formal diplomatic notes, custom does not require their publication. . . . The Kennedy-

*President Kennedy and Soviet leader Nikita Krushchev, the two key figures in the 1962 Cuban missile crisis in which the United States forced the Soviet Union to remove nuclear weapons from Cuba.*

Khrushchev notes were not a substitute for normal diplomatic endeavor, but a supplement, resorted to when the diplomats were unable to agree or when the problem exceeded the bounds of the forum in which they were negotiating.

## To recognize or not to recognize?

The president has still another way to create foreign policy without including Congress in the process. This is through his ability to recognize, or refrain from recognizing, foreign governments. Presidents have regularly cited the constitutional provision that the president shall "receive Ambassadors and other public Ministers" as the basis of their power to recognize or not recognize the legitimacy of other nations. Because it can instantly establish a long-lasting and complex relationship between the United States and another country, presidential recognition is a powerful form of foreign policy. Not surprisingly, many presidents have used such recognition to further their aims. One of the clearest examples occurred in 1903, after the South American nation of Colombia refused to grant the United States the right to build a canal across the isthmus of Panama, then Colombian territory. Theodore Roosevelt promptly backed a revolutionary movement in Panama and formally recognized the independent nation of Panama. Only weeks later, Roosevelt signed a treaty with the new country granting the United States its right to build the canal.

Because of U.S. superpower status in the post–World War II world, U.S. recognition has also led the way for other nations to recognize controversial new countries. For instance in 1948, Jewish settlers in the Middle East declared the establishment of the new nation of Israel. A number

*President Truman meets with Chaim Weizmann, provisional president of Israel, shortly after the nation's creation. Truman was the first to recognize Israel's status as a nation.*

of other nations disputed Israel's legitimacy on the grounds that it had usurped lands belonging to other countries. President Harry Truman boldly recognized Israel. This not only founded a warm and lasting relationship between the two countries, but also made many other nations more comfortable about recognizing Israel.

On the flip side, the president can create significant foreign policy by withholding official recognition. In 1991, for example, military leaders in the Caribbean nation of Haiti ousted the elected president, Jean-Bertrand Aristide. President Bush refused to recognize the Haitian rebels' government. This established that government as an outlaw regime in the world's eyes, and many nations cut off aid to and trade with Haiti. President Clinton continued Bush's policy of nonrecognition of the Haitian rebels.

*President Clinton meets with exiled Haitian president Jean-Bertrand Aristide in 1993.*

By withholding recognition of Haiti's military government, and by exerting diplomatic and economic pressure on the regime, Clinton hoped to drive the military leaders from power. At the same time, he refused to rule out the possibility of a military invasion. The threat of invasion prompted a congressional resolution calling for the president to notify Congress before ordering troops to Haiti. Such resolutions are nonbinding, meaning that presidents have no legal obligation to follow them. Although the resolution, sponsored by Senator Bob Dole of Kansas did not pass, polls at the time showed that a majority of Americans opposed military intervention in Haiti. This added strength and a moral edge to the congressional resolution.

*At President Clinton's order, U.S. troops enter Haiti. Using diplomacy and the threat of military force, Clinton helped Aristide return to Haiti and resume his office in October 1994.*

Nevertheless, Clinton dispatched fifteen thousand U.S. troops to Haiti in September 1994 without seeking congressional approval. Although last-minute negotiations allowed U.S. troops to enter Haiti peacefully, Clinton's actions reignited the debate over Congress's powers in the areas of war and foreign affairs. By that time, however, Congress had little option but to offer support for American forces and urge their speedy return. Once again, Congress's weakness in the area of foreign policy was revealed.

For the most part, the history of U.S. foreign policy has seen presidents act and Congress react. This situation is not likely to change in the foreseeable future. The U.S. presidency retains and freely utilizes many firm advantages. These include superior information sources, instant access to the world media, unlimited use of executive agreements, and the unique abilities to make sweeping policy statements, engage in secret diplomacy, and recognize foreign countries. As long as the president maintains these and the other advantages that his special office affords him, he will remain the nation's major foreign policy voice.

# 6

# Presidential Appointments

THE AUTHORITY TO appoint judges, cabinet secretaries, diplomats, and other officials is one of the president's most important powers. Because such officials are not elected, the people trust the chief executive to select competent and effective persons to fill important government positions. The cabinet personnel the president chooses make daily decisions that affect the lives of millions of Americans. And appointed foreign ambassadors, as the people's representatives abroad, help shape the way foreigners view the United States. The president's power to nominate judges to the Supreme Court is particularly significant. Because a judge is appointed for life, he or she usually continues to make decisions profoundly affecting society long after his or her presidential sponsor has left office.

## The division of authority

In all, a modern president assuming office appoints or nominates for appointment over five thousand officials of various kinds, far more than in any other democratic nation. Because of the sweeping nature of the appointive power, the possibility always exists, of course, that a president

*(Opposite page) President Bush (right) stands with Clarence Thomas shortly after nominating Thomas to the Supreme Court. Court judges and other officials appointed by the president make decisions that affect millions of people in the United States and around the world.*

103

might abuse such authority. Or he simply might consistently make poor choices. A review of U.S. history reveals a number of examples of each of these scenarios. In order to guard against such incidents, Congress acts as a kind of watchdog over many presidential appointments. Some appointees, such as those for the Supreme Court, must receive congressional approval before getting the job. Even in cases where no approval is necessary, the legislature can, through widely publicized investigations, force a president to rethink an appointment or fire someone already appointed.

This division of authority regarding appointments, like other aspects of the executive-legislative rivalry, harks back to the 1787 Constitutional Convention. As they did in other areas of government, the founders made sure to divide appointive authority between the president and Congress. James Pfiffner explains:

> The Framers of the Constitution were greatly concerned with the quality of those chosen to run the government, feeling that their character would determine the overall quality of the U.S. government. Those Framers favoring a strong executive wanted to give the president exclusive authority to make appointments. But those distrustful of executive power preferred to give the appointment power to the Senate. At the end of the Constitutional Convention the issue was finally settled by the compromise calling for presidential nomination and Senate confirmation of the major appointments to the executive [and judicial branches].

In general, those appointed offices requiring senatorial approval are referred to as "superior" offices and include Supreme Court judges, cabinet secretaries, and heads of various government departments.

Congress has been especially watchful and selective about superior presidential appointments

in the second half of the twentieth century. This is because the United States emerged in this period as the leading nation in a modern, complex world. The great power and influence possessed by superior appointees makes them key figures, sometimes on a global scale. So Congress carefully considers each such appointee and quickly challenges a president if it finds fault with his choice.

*The members of the U.S. Supreme Court in 1993. Because they wield such great power and influence, Congress carefully scrutinizes their appointments.*

## Parties and patronage

By contrast, friction between president and Congress over appointments was far less frequent and intense in the country's early decades. This was because the infant U.S. government was small and the number of appointments relatively few. Also, the first few presidents almost always appointed respected, upper-class men who, prevailing opinion held, were largely capable and trustworthy. Thus, with few exceptions, the early selection process centered less on congressional participation and more on the individual judgment of each president.

At first, presidents found selecting the modest number of appointees and nominees a relatively small-scale process. But as the country quickly expanded in the early 1800s, the government also grew in size. Presidents eventually faced the daunting task of choosing hundreds of people to fill various government job vacancies. In time, this task came to be dominated by the political parties, which used the patronage system. Under the unwritten rules of patronage, when a party's candidate won an election, those faithful party members who had worked hard for the candidate expected to be rewarded with government jobs. Before the development of the modern presidency in the mid-twentieth century, the patronage system generated the majority of presidential appointments.

## Abuse of the patronage system

Most presidents did not severely abuse the patronage system's granting of rewards for loyalty. Even those appointees who were not particularly talented or memorable generally proved to be at least competent. Exceptions occurred, of course, the most notable in President Warren Harding's administration in the early 1920s. Most of his major cabinet officials were incompetent and corrupt individuals chosen because they had earlier been friends with or done favors for the president. These men brought both the patronage system and the presidency to their lowest levels.

It is worth noting that abuses of the rewards system did not always involve incompetent individuals. When the 1824 election ended up in the

House because no candidate received a majority of electoral votes, second-place finisher John Quincy Adams struck a deal with fourth-place finisher Henry Clay. In exchange for his support, Adams promised Clay the position of secretary of state. Clay agreed and backed Adams, Adams became president, and, per the deal, Clay became secretary of state. Clay was a highly talented and experienced politician. Nevertheless, this extreme version of patronage was seen as underhanded and widely condemned.

Eventually, the role of party patronage in the selection of presidential appointments declined. This was partly due to the rise of the primary election process in the twentieth century. When control of the presidential nominating process shifted from party bosses to the people, presidents owed fewer favors to the bosses and other party

*President Warren Harding (left) and his cabinet members pose for a picture in the early 1920s. Many of Harding's appointees turned out to be corrupt or incompetent.*

faithful. Another factor was the rise of the White House recruitment staff. By the 1940s and 1950s, presidential appointments numbered in the thousands, and incoming chief executives employed more and more full-time staffers to search out prospective appointees. John Kennedy had a recruitment staff of 3, Richard Nixon of 30 to 40, Ronald Reagan of about 100, and Bill Clinton of at least 130. Although loyalty to party and candidate still plays some part in the appointive process, recruiters now tend to focus more on a potential appointee's background and ability.

In fact, background has become an increasingly important criterion in choosing high appointees, such as those for cabinet or Supreme Court positions. In the past, consideration of background was usually limited to a candidate's prior political

*Once sworn in as a Supreme Court justice, Salmon P. Chase, a Lincoln appointee, did not always support the president's policies.*

leanings. The person's tendency to support a certain idea or cause—be it liberal, conservative, or otherwise—often made him or her an attractive candidate. For example, Abraham Lincoln nominated Salmon P. Chase as chief justice of the Supreme Court mainly because Chase, as former secretary of the treasury, had supported an issue involving paper money. And Woodrow Wilson appointed Louis D. Brandeis to the high court partly because of his ideas on antitrust law. Both of these cases showed how such strategy can and often does backfire. Once on the Court, Chase did not support Lincoln's position on the paper money issue, and Brandeis wrote only a single decision on antitrust law.

*Thurgood Marshall, appointed by Lyndon Johnson in 1967, was the first African American on the Supreme Court.*

## Increased political participation

In any case, political orientation tended to be the main background criterion of appointees as long as everyone expected selection to be restricted, as it was for so long, to white males. Beginning in the 1960s, however, major social changes in the country opened the way for increased political participation by women and racial minorities. A person's background was now seen to include not only prior liberal or conservative leanings, but also gender, race, and ethnicity. Seeking to gain or maintain popular support, presidents were quick to use these new criteria in choosing nominees. In the midst of the great civil rights advances of the late 1960s, for instance, Lyndon Johnson appointed Thurgood Marshall, the first African American ever to sit on the Supreme Court. When Marshall resigned in 1991, George Bush bowed to public opinion that favored maintaining a racial balance on the Court. He nominated another African American, federal judge Clarence Thomas, whom the Senate confirmed later that year.

*President Reagan confers with Arizona judge Sandra Day O'Connor, his 1981 appointee to the Supreme Court. O'Connor became the first woman to sit on the high court.*

Similarly, with the rise of the women's movement in the 1970s and 1980s, Ronald Reagan saw the political wisdom of nominating a woman to the high court. He chose Arizona judge Sandra Day O'Connor, who became the first female Supreme Court justice in September 1981. However, Reagan's strategy in selecting O'Connor was twofold. He wanted not only to address the concerns of women, who constitute half the voters, but also to further his conservative political agenda. According to Forrest McDonald:

> When Ronald Reagan assumed the presidency in 1981, checking the [liberal] tendencies of the Court was high on his agenda. He . . . scrupulously [carefully] screened prospective nominees for ability and integrity, but more importantly for judicial

philosophy, the idea being to appoint people who believed in judicial restraint [making conservative decisions].

In 1993, Bill Clinton used the same strategy to further his own political agenda. He appointed Ruth Bader Ginsberg to be the second woman on the Supreme Court and thereby exhibited his respect and support for qualified women in government. His other reason for choosing Ginsberg was her strong liberal philosophy. In this way, as presidents of different political persuasions come and go, they leave their lasting philosophical mark upon the nation's highest court.

*Bill Clinton walks with Judge Ruth Bader Ginsberg, whom he appointed to the Supreme Court in 1993.*

Despite their varied backgrounds, Marshall, Thomas, O'Connor, and Ginsberg shared an experience common to all modern presidential appointees to superior offices. They all underwent intense congressional scrutiny that exposed the events and details of their lives to the media and the public. In contrast to the country's first years, when it exercised its watchdog role less forcefully, Congress now sharply examines each superior appointment and frequently challenges presidential choices.

A prominent recent example was congressional refusal to confirm John G. Tower of Texas, President Bush's nominee for the crucial office of secretary of defense. On March 9, 1989, the Senate voted 53 to 47 to reject Tower, the first cabinet nominee denied approval in thirty years and only the fifteenth such nominee rejected between 1789

*Texas politician John Tower was rejected by the Senate in 1989 after President Bush nominated him for the post of secretary of defense.*

*Lani Guinier of Pennsylvania, whose 1993 nomination to be head of the Justice Department's Civil Rights Division was withdrawn by President Clinton.*

and 1990. Many legislators cited reports of drinking problems in their rejection of Tower. The nominee's insistence that he had "never been an alcoholic or dependent on alcohol" and his public pledge that if confirmed he would refrain from drinking for his whole term as secretary did not sway the Senate.

Sometimes initial congressional disapproval of a nominee and the resulting negative media attention are unusually intense. In such cases, presidents may withdraw the nominee rather than face an embarrassing rejection vote in the Senate. This has happened several times to Bill Clinton. In 1993, for example, Clinton withdrew University of Pennsylvania law professor Lani Guinier from consideration as head of the Justice Department's Civil Rights Division. Many legislators complained that her views on civil rights were too militant.

*G. Harrold Carswell, a Nixon appointee to the Supreme Court. The Senate rejected Carswell in 1970 on the grounds that some of his prior writings had displayed a racial bias against blacks.*

Executive-legislative fights over Supreme Court nominees tend to be even more widely publicized and controversial. From 1789 to the present, the Senate rejected only twenty-seven such nominees and each case proved to be a dramatic confrontation between president and Congress. The reasons for these rejections varied considerably. In the case of G. Harrold Carswell, one of Richard Nixon's Supreme Court nominees, the charges were that the candidate was racist. Nixon nominated Carswell in January 1970 and, according to political scientist James D. Barber,

> by March 1970 the nominee, and by implication his insistent nominator [Nixon], were in big trouble. . . . With the leadership of Senator Birch Bayh [of Indiana], a host of civil rights and other liberal forces had independently dug into Carswell's record, discovering he had (long ago) spoken out for white supremacy, that he [belonged to] a whites-only country club, that he had harassed black plaintiffs and their attorneys. . . . A massive drive to defeat Carswell began: the petitions and

letters from law school deans, professors, and civil rights groups poured in, accentuating the negative.

Nixon stubbornly stuck by Carswell. The president also made a number of ill-conceived public statements questioning the legislators' judgment and their right to challenge his authority. Not surprisingly, the Senate, partly in response to Nixon's attacks, rejected Carswell on April 8, 1970.

Some of the more recent cases were just as controversial. In June 1987, for example, Ronald Reagan nominated District of Columbia judge Robert H. Bork to the high court. Many legislators claimed that an examination of Bork's record as a judge showed that he was far too conservative on certain controversial issues. In their view, if confirmed, Bork might make decisions that threatened such cherished American rights as

*President Reagan stands with his Supreme Court nominee, Robert H. Bork, in 1987, shortly before the Senate rejected Bork because of his conservative views.*

those guaranteeing free speech and privacy. In October of the same year, the Senate rejected Bork by a vote of 58 to 42. Reagan experienced further frustration in the following weeks. Six days after Bork's rejection, the president nominated another conservative judge—Douglas H. Ginsberg. Pressured by intense congressional and media scrutiny, Ginsberg withdrew himself from contention a few days later after admitting to charges that he had smoked marijuana in his youth. The Senate finally accepted Reagan's third nominee, Anthony M. Kennedy of California.

## People get what they deserve

Such confrontations between presidents and legislators over appointments—like those over legislation, war powers, and foreign affairs—are

*Judge Douglas H. Ginsberg, another Reagan Supreme Court appointee, withdrew himself from consideration only a few days after being nominated.*

more than just battles among politicians. In the United States, the world's oldest and largest democracy, the people elect all of these leaders. Because they act in the name of and for the good of the people, their battles must be viewed as the people's battles. In that context, the public bears the ultimate responsibility for selecting capable and trustworthy leaders. Many persons are quick to blame the sitting president for bad times, for inept mistakes, or for corrupt actions. But just as many often forget that presidential character is usually a reflection of the national character. Only a literate, hardworking, honest, and concerned populace will choose a president with these same attributes. As Marcus Cunliffe so aptly puts it:

> The nation gets the president it deserves. An America obsessed with popularity ratings will pick a chief executive because he looks the part—and get a man who in turn is obsessed with popularity ratings. A brutal nation merits a brutal executive. A complacent, mindless country ought not to be surprised if the White House is occupied by a . . . bore. Only if Americans seek and value excellence in their own lives have they the right to hope for an excellent president.

# Glossary

**adjourn**: To close a meeting or session.

**amendment**: A change or addition to a law or legislative bill.

**appointive power**: The authority to appoint people to government posts.

**bill**: A proposed law or other legislative measure.

**cabinet**: A president's chief department heads.

**caucus**: A political meeting, usually held in private.

**chief executive**: A nation's president or highest ranking administrator.

**civilian supremacy**: The state of affairs in which a civilian has command of a country's military forces.

**civil rights**: A broad range of rights, freedoms, and privileges granted by the U.S. Constitution.

**conservative**: In politics, tending to follow established tradition and styles, and therefore to be cautious and slower to change.

**constituent**: A citizen who is represented in a government by the officials for whom he or she votes.

**draft**: In the legislative process, to write a detailed version of a bill.

**executive agreement**: A foreign accord negotiated by the president without ratification or other participation by Congress; essentially, executive agreements can accomplish the same objectives as treaties.

**executive branch**: The government wing that consists of the president, vice president, and the president's cabinet.

**federal**: Having a national, as opposed to state or local, nature or jurisdiction.

**incumbent**: Currently "sitting," or serving, in office.

**joint chiefs**: The heads of the various armed service branches.

**legislative presidency**: A term describing the strong legislative leadership role assumed by most modern presidents.

**liberal**: In politics, tending to try, as well as to tolerate, new ideas and approaches, and therefore to be quicker to change.

**oligarchy**: A government run by a small group of powerful individuals.

**patronage system**: The political method of rewarding former favors, loyalty, or other support through the granting of government jobs.

**plurality**: In a contest of more than two candidates, the number of votes cast for the winner if this number is less than half the total votes cast.

**police actions**: Military operations ordered by a president to protect American lives and property or to punish those who threaten them.

**primary election**: A preliminary election in which the voters of a state choose presidential nominees either by direct ballot or by choosing delegates who, in turn, will choose the candidates at the national conventions.

**ratify**: To approve.

**representative legislature**: A lawmaking body composed of members who represent the people.

**shared powers**: Those constitutional powers divided variously among the government branches.

**superior appointments**: Presidential appointments to high and important offices such as those in the cabinet and Supreme Court.

**treaty**: A major foreign agreement that ends a war, forms an alliance, decides a territorial dispute, or establishes some other kind of relationship between two or more countries.

**veto**: The president's power to reject a bill submitted by Congress.

**war powers**: The constitutional authorizations to wage war, which are divided between the president and Congress.

# Suggestions for Further Reading

Ralph K. Andrist, *Andrew Jackson: Soldier and Statesman.* New York: American Heritage, 1963.

Carl S. Anthony, *America's Most Influential First Ladies.* Minneapolis: Oliver Press, 1992.

Isaac Asimov, *The Birth of the United States: 1763–1816.* Boston: Houghton Mifflin, 1974.

Harold Coy, *The First Book of Presidents.* New York: Franklin Watts, 1981.

Louis Fisher, *Constitutional Conflicts Between Congress and the President.* Princeton, NJ: Princeton University Press, 1985.

J. Perry Leavell Jr., *Woodrow Wilson.* New York: Chelsea House, 1987.

Don Nardo, *Franklin D. Roosevelt.* New York: Chelsea House, 1995.

Don Nardo, *The Importance of Thomas Jefferson.* San Diego: Lucent Books, 1993.

Don Nardo, *The U.S. Congress.* San Diego: Lucent Books, 1994.

Diane Ravitch and Abigail Thernstrom, eds., *The Democracy Reader.* New York: HarperCollins, 1992.

Peter Lars Sandberg, *Dwight D. Eisenhower.* New York: Chelsea House, 1986.

Irwin Unger, *These United States: The Questions of Our Past.* Boston: Little, Brown, 1978.

Brian Williams, *George Washington.* New York: Marshall Cavendish, 1988.

# Works Consulted

James D. Barber, *The Presidential Character: Predicting Performance in the White House.* Englewood Cliffs, NJ: Prentice-Hall, 1972.

Wilfred E. Binkley, *President and Congress.* New York: Random House, 1962.

Paul F. Boller Jr., *Presidential Anecdotes.* New York: Oxford University Press, 1981.

Marcus Cunliffe, *American Presidents and the Presidency.* London: Eyre and Spottiswoode, 1968.

Erwin C. Hargrove, *The Power of the Modern Presidency.* Philadelphia: Temple University Press, 1974.

Emmet John Hughes, *The Living Presidency.* New York: Coward, McCann, and Geoghegan, 1973.

Louis W. Koenig, *The Chief Executive.* New York: Harcourt, Brace, and World, 1964.

Forrest McDonald, *The American Presidency: An Intellectual History.* Lawrence: University Press of Kansas, 1994.

Neal R. Peirce, *The People's President: The Electoral College in American History and the Direct-Vote Alternative.* New York: Simon and Schuster, 1968.

James P. Pfiffner, *The Modern Presidency.* New York: St. Martin's Press, 1994.

Richard M. Pious, *The American Presidency.* New York: Basic Books, 1979.

Albert B. Saye et al., *Principles of American Government.* Englewood Cliffs, NJ: Prentice-Hall, 1970.

Malcolm Shaw, ed., *The Modern Presidency: From Roosevelt to Reagan.* New York: Harper and Row, 1987.

Sidney Warren, ed., *The American President.* Englewood Cliffs, NJ: Prentice-Hall, 1967.

# Index

# About the Author

Don Nardo is an award-winning author whose more than fifty books cover a wide range of topics. Among his many science-related works are *Medical Diagnosis, Lasers, Gravity, Germs, Vaccines, Vitamins and Minerals*, and two volumes on dinosaurs. His five books covering American wars include *The Mexican-American War*, *The Indian Wars*, and *The Persian Gulf War*, and among his other historical studies are *Ancient Greece*, *The Roman Republic*, *The Roman Empire*, *Greek and Roman Theater*, and a two-volume history of Japan. This volume on the presidency is a companion piece to his other works on government: *Democracy*, *The U.S. Congress*, and biographies of Thomas Jefferson and Franklin D. Roosevelt. Mr. Nardo, who has also written numerous screenplays and teleplays, including work for Warner Brothers and ABC-Television, lives with his wife, Christine, on Cape Cod, Massachusetts.

# Picture Credits

Cover photo by James Colburn/Photoreporters

AP/Wide World Photos, 12, 82, 86

The Bettmann Archive, 20, 22, 32, 48, 77 (top)

Mary Anne Fackelman-Miner/The White House, 67

FDR Library, 63

Library of Congress, 13, 17, 21, 25, 27, 28 (both), 31, 37, 38, 40, 41, 42, 43, 46, 54, 56, 57, 59, 60, 62, 66, 71, 72, 75, 77 (bottom), 79, 94, 95, 107, 108

National Archives, 23, 81, 89, 90

North Wind Picture Archives, 11, 19

Reuters/Bettmann, 6, 50, 61, 84, 99, 100, 105, 111, 113

Stock Montage, Inc., 26

UPI/Bettmann, 9, 14, 34, 45, 64, 78, 83, 91, 97, 98, 102, 109, 110, 112, 114, 115, 116

U.S. Army, courtesy Harry S Truman Library, 73

*Copyright Washington Post; Reprinted by permission of the D.C. Public Library*, 10, 47, 49, 68, 93